# Coconut Oil
## for A Healthy Planet

**A Sustainable Natural Resource that Saves Lives and Protects the Environment**

## Bruce Fife, ND

Piccadilly Books, Ltd.
Colorado Springs, CO

Every effort has been made to ensure that the information contained in this book is complete and accurate. However, neither the publisher nor the author is engaged in rendering professional advice or services to the individual reader. The ideas and suggestions contained in this book are not intended as a substitute for consulting with your physician. Neither the publisher nor the author are responsible for your specific health or allergy needs.

Photo credits: page 18 Naomi Dilodilo, MD; pages 24, 26, 27, 33, 34, 38, 56, 57, 71, 75, 105 Wikipedia commons; page 39 *The Guardian*, Abraham Diaz; page 45 CocoTherapy; page 49 AquaBounty Technologies; pages 90, 93, 94, 95 Kokonut Pacific; pages 98, 99, 100, 101 Elizabeth Wangari Gachiri; page 104 US Fish and Wildlife Service; page 107 National Oceanic and Atmospheric Administration (NOAA).

**Piccadilly Books, Ltd.**
**P.O. Box 25203**
**Colorado Springs, CO 80936, USA**
**info@piccadillybooks.com**
**www.piccadillybooks.com**

ISBN 9781691281459

# Contents

Chapter 1: **The Coconut Oil Miracle** .......................... 5

Chapter 2: **1001 Uses for Coconut Oil** ...................... 21

Chapter 3: **A Sustainable Natural Resource** ............... 48

Chapter 4: **A Clean All-Purpose Industrial Oil** ......... 77

Chapter 5: **Changing People's Lives** ........................ 87

Chapter 6: **Protecting Marine Life** .......................103

Appendix: **The Coconut Bookshelf** ...................... 111

About the Author ....................................... 135

References ............................................. 136

# 1

# The Coconut Oil Miracle

## HOW I DISCOVERED COCONUT OIL

Did you know that 1.27 billion children live in poverty—deprived of food, safe drinking water, healthcare or shelter?

Could you imagine being unemployed, homeless, and forced to beg in the streets for food? Not a pleasant thought is it? But this is the life many people face throughout the world. Millions of poverty stricken children and their families go to bed hungry each night not knowing where their next meal is coming from. Often, it is found in the refuge discarded by others as unfit to eat. Half naked children as young as 3 and 4 years of age roam the streets begging for food. If you live in an affluent country like the US, sights like this are rare, but in Third World counties they are common.

The plight of these people was made clearly evident to me when I made my first trip to Asia in 2004. My heart went out to the many underweight and malnourished children begging for food. No one should be forced to live like this, I thought. I wanted to help, but how? How could one person help so many in need? By myself I could do little. This was a global issue. The solution would require a global effort—a task far beyond my limited capability. I felt helpless.

Although I didn't realize it at first, the answer to the problem, or at least a partial answer, was staring me right in the face. The solution? It was simple—coconut. Yes, coconut was the answer. The reason I had come to Asia was to teach the people about the nutritional and medicinal benefits of coconut. This is an abundant and renewable, natural resource that has been vastly underdeveloped.

Without realizing it, I had been working on the answer for some time. Like most everyone else, I used to believe that coconut, especially coconut oil, was unhealthy because it was high in saturated fat. But then I had an experience that changed the way I think about fats and oils and particularly about coconut oil. Some years ago a colleague of mine, a nutritionist, told me that coconut oil was one of the good fats, that it did not cause heart disease, and that it had many health benefits. At first, I was shocked. This went against everything I had ever read in the newspaper and in the popular diet books. But this nutritionist showed me some studies that indicated that coconut oil had many important nutritional and medical uses. Coconut oil, in one form or another, was used in hospital IV solutions, it was added to infant formula, and used in anti-candida medications. I became curious. If coconut oil had so many nutritional and medical uses why is it considered a dietary nightmare? If it did cause heart disease why is it used in hospital IV solutions and given to newborn babies. It just didn't make sense. I had to find the answer.

Since everyone seemed to know that coconut oil caused heart disease I was certain that there must be many magazine articles written on the subject. Many of which would outline the dangers of using coconut oil and cite references to studies backing up these claims. So I went on a search to find some of these articles. I went on the Internet and to the library and looked for everything I could on coconut oil. At that time, mid-1990s, there wasn't anything written specifically about coconut oil. Now I did find many articles on nutrition and dietary oils, and most of them did contain one sentence about coconut oil and that sentence was exactly alike in all of them. It was, "Coconut oil is a saturated fat and causes heart disease." I ran across that statement over and over again. I still see that very same statement repeated now. It was like there was a royal decree that went out throughout the land dictating that if anyone wrote anything about nutrition they must include this statement on coconut oil—it's the politically correct thing to do.

Even though I ran across this statement time and time again, not once did any of these authors ever back up that statement with any facts, any figures, or any citations to the medical studies. There weren't even any anecdotal accounts. When I started this search I fully expected to read stories where people had used coconut oil since they were little children and by the time they were 30 years old they had raging heart disease. But there wasn't anything like that. It became obvious to me that these doctors and nutritionists who were writing these things knew absolutely nothing about coconut oil. All they were doing was repeating what someone else had said, who in turn, was just repeating what someone else said before them, and on and on. None of them bothered to do their own research but just blindly accepted what others were saying.

It became apparent to me that if I was going to learn the truth about coconut oil, I wasn't going to find it in health books and magazine articles because none of these authors knew anything about it. If I was going to learn the truth I was going to have to go to the medical studies and see what researchers were actually discovering. That's what I did. In my search through the medical literature I found hundreds of research articles on coconut. And what I found shocked me. I discovered why coconut oil, in one form or another, was used in hospital IV solutions, why it was added to infant formula, and was used in anti-candida medications. I also learned it was recommended for those with digestive concerns, and that it could help prevent a wide variety of health problems ranging from cancer and diabetes to influenza and AIDS. I was amazed! I also learned that there was absolutely no truth whatsoever in the belief that coconut oil causes or even contributes to heart disease. I failed to find even a single study that proved that coconut oil consumption caused heart disease. No such study exists. In fact, what I learned was that coconut oil can help prevent heart disease!

I learned that coconut oil has had a long history of use throughout the world as both a food and as a medicine. People in coconut growing regions of the world have been using it for thousands of years without suffering from heart disease. In fact, those people who use coconut oil as their primary source of fat have very lower rates of heart disease.

## THE ECONOMIC IMPACT OF THE
## ANTI-COCONUT OIL CAMPAIGN

The truth of the matter is that if you want to protect yourself from heart disease, you should be using coconut oil. What an incredible discovery! So why had we been told that coconut oil causes heart disease? The answer is a combination of misconception, ignorance, and greed.

Since the 1950s it was observed that some saturated fats tend to raise blood cholesterol. Since cholesterol levels were considered a risk factor for heart disease doctors were recommending that we reduce our saturated fat intake. The vegetable oil industry promoted this idea very aggressively in order to influence people to use vegetable oil in place of saturated fats. Since the tropical oils (coconut and palm) were highly saturated they were viewed as being unhealthy and even a cause heart disease, even though no study had ever shown it.

Up until the mid-1980s coconut oil was commonly used in many foods in North America. The anti-saturated fat campaigns sponsored by the soybean industry and misguided special interest groups succeeded in frightening the public away from using coconut oil and food manufacturers and restaurants eventually replaced it with hydrogenated soybean oil. By 1990 coconut had virtually disappeared from American and European diets. Even in coconut growing regions of the world, such as Malaysia and the Philippines, coconut oil was viewed as an artery-clogging fat and largely avoided. As a consequence, demand for coconut products plummeted and the coconut industry fell into a deep depression that lasted for two decades. Coconut farmers unable to sell their products stopped harvesting. Literally millions of farmers, pickers, consolidators, truckers, and processors were no longer able to earn a living. Many took on other jobs, if they could find them. Others continued working in the coconut industry because other jobs were unavailable. They barely eked out a living year by year on a pauper's wage. Many out of work and underemployed parents could not properly feed and clothe their children. They turned to begging in the streets.

The connection between heart disease and coconut oil that frightened so many people never existed. What most people didn't understand at the time was that there are many different types of saturated fat and that the fat in coconut oil is completely different from that found in animal fats or other vegetable oils (all fats and oils from both animals and plants contain a mixture of saturated and unsaturated fats). This difference is important because it's what makes coconut oil unique and gives it its remarkable healing properties.

As I learned about the healing potential of coconut oil I began using it myself and recommended it to others. I saw it clear up hemorrhoids, stop bladder infections, remove cancerous skin lesions, reverse the effects of hypothyroidism and diabetes, and help people lose excess weight, improve digestive function, among other things. There seemed to be no end to the miracles it could do.

## A BOLD STEP

After learning all of this, I realized that few people outside of the research community knew about the healing miracles of coconut oil. I felt an obligation to share this knowledge with others, so I wrote the book *The Coconut Oil Miracle*. All of the information in that book came directly from the medical literature and my own experience. Everything I stated was backed by medical studies, many of which were cited in the book. I purposely wrote it in easy-to-understand language so that the laymen could understand.

When I finished the manuscript I gave it to Jon J. Kabara, PhD, a prominent lipid researcher and professor of chemistry and pharmacology at Michigan State University, and asked him to review it for accuracy and content. He praised the book but then added, "Don't publish it."

I was shocked. "Why? It's accurate isn't it?"

"Yes," he replied, "but nobody will read it. If you publish this book you'll just be wasting your time and money."

He spoke from experience. He had known about the benefits of coconut oil for years, whenever he spoke favorably about coconut oil he was either ignored or ridiculed. He learned to keep silent.

He was trying to protect me from criticism as well as wasting my money in financing the publication of the book. Despite his warning, I felt a need to get this information out to the public. The health benefits of coconut were so remarkable that I couldn't keep this knowledge locked away in research journals, inaccessible to the average person. I decided that even if the book didn't sell, at least I could say I tried. Because coconut oil offered so many health benefits I felt confident that if the facts were presented in a logical, easy-to-read format, backed by decades of medical research, the book would find a receptive audience, even if only a small one.

Because the book went against the prevailing opinion about fats, I knew from the start that I would face criticism

10

and ridicule. That didn't stop me. As I think back on it now, it was a bold and crazy move on my part. Why would anyone knowingly publish a book that would generate scorn? I just felt a need to share this knowledge despite the risks.

I didn't bother to send the manuscript to an established publisher because I knew none of them would dare touch it—too risky for them. Finding money to publish the book myself was another problem. It would require several thousand dollars. Money I just didn't have at the time. So I began to save. I tightened our family's budget. We ate more economically and cut corners, reducing expenses to a bare minimum.

At first, sales were slow. The title scared people away. Stores didn't want to stock it. Few could accept the idea that coconut oil was healthy. People thought I was crazy. A few people laughed at me thinking the book was a joke. Some were even angered that I would publish such a book and criticized me. Articles in newspapers and health newsletters reemphasized the politically correct, but inaccurate, perception of coconut oil and raked me across the coals with false accusations in an attempt to ruin my credibility.

My saving grace was that if I could get someone to just read the book and see the evidence for themselves, they generally become converted. I let the facts speak for themselves. This was clearly demonstrated to me by an incident that occurred soon after the book was published. I gave a copy to one of my neighbors. Cautiously he took the book and with skepticism promised to read it. He became an immediate convert. He was so enthusiastic about the potential of coconut oil that he began telling others about it. He went to his nutritionist and showed her the book. When she saw it she scoffed, "That's just somebody's opinion. Coconut oil is no good," she said. She refused to even look at it.

He begged her to read the book and give it a fair trial. Hesitantly she consented. He placed the book on her desk and left. The following week he returned to her office and found the book positioned exactly where he had left it. Obviously she had not even touched the book. Again he insisted that she read it. Again she objected, but eventually gave in. Before leaving he made her promise that she would read it by the time he returned. To keep him off her back she reluctantly agreed.

When she started to read the book she was immediately impressed by the logical and approach and the abundance of medical references that backed up each statement. She devoured the book in two days. She wanted to know more. She contacted me and we had many discussions about fats and oils. I opened her eyes. She changed her approach to nutritional counseling and began recommending the book to all of her patients. That's what happens when people read the book. They become excited and tell others. Those who criticize me or the book do so because they haven't read it. They are too closed-minded.

At first I found it impossible to get any media coverage or book reviews. No one in the media would touch it. The book began selling by word of mouth and interest slowly grew. People began using the oil and experiencing changes. Many people with chronic health problems found relief. Personal testimonials encouraged others to read the book. As interest grew I was able to get more notice in newspapers and magazines. Several excellent articles appeared in national magazines. Demand for good quality coconut oil was rapidly increasing. Because people wanted the oil for health reasons they were going to health food stores to look for it. When the book was first published coconut oil was almost impossible to find anywhere. Very few stores carried it and when they did, it was always in the cosmetic section and sold as a body oil. Today nearly every health food store and most grocery stores in North American as well as many pharmacies stock food grade coconut oil. Some carry as many as 5 or 6 different brands. Coconut oil has now come out of the closet and is staking its rightful claim as "the healthiest oil on earth."

Since the publication of that book in 2000, I've written more than 14 additional books that describe the health, nutritional, and culinary benefits and uses of coconut oil and other coconut products. These books have been published in dozens of languages. I now travel the world lecturing at medical schools, universities, trade shows, health conferences, hospitals, spas, and elsewhere. For this reason, I have gained an international reputation as "the" coconut expert and have respectfully been given the moniker "Dr. Coconut."

## LIVES ARE BEING CHANGED

As a result of the increased demand for coconut products, the coconut industry has experienced a resurrection. Coconut farmers are finding new markets for their products, laborers are finding much needed jobs collecting and harvesting. Coconut processing plants that had remained silent or underutilized for two decades are now operating at full capacity. People are finding employment. Children who were forced to beg in the streets are now being fed and clothed and receiving medical attention. These people are finding hope.

When I first published *The Coconut Oil Miracle*, my main purpose was to tell everyone about the health benefits they could enjoy by using the oil. After the book started to sell I was only partially aware that it helped to fuel the economic resurgence of the coconut industry in many Third World countries. When I was invited by the Philippine Department of Trade and Industry to come to Manila and lecture on the health benefits of coconut, I saw first-hand the remarkable impact my book had on the economy and the coconut industry. Many people came up to me to shake my hand and express gratitude saying, "Because of you I am able to provide for my family. God bless you."

Even medical professionals were eager to meet me. One of which was Naomi Dilodilo, MD. She sent me an e-mail with the greeting "Biyaya" and said, "This means blessing

*Philippine president Gloria Macapagal-Arroyo with Agriculture Secretary Arthur Yap acknowledges the efforts of author Bruce Fife (with wife Leslie) in dispelling decades of misinformation about coconut and helping revive the coconut industry in the Philippines, which provides for the livelihoods of over 20 million people in that country. Dr. Fife presented president Macapagal-Arroyo with a copy of his book Coconut Cures.*

and you are one! You have been a channel of blessings to millions of Filipinos, one third of the population of which is directly dependent on the coconuts for their livelihood... Thank you very much for all your efforts and contribution to the coconut oil information campaign. I, as a Filipino, appreciate very much your endeavors. It means a lot to us. 'Salamat' is thank you in our language and comes deep from my heart!" Wow, what a response. I was humbled. Little did I know the impact my book would have.

In the Philippines alone at least 20 million people depend on coconut for their livelihoods. There are millions more in Indonesia, Malaysia, India, Sri Lanka, and other countries. In Fiji, Samoa, and other islands coconut production accounts to up to 75 percent of their income. Approximately 100 million people worldwide are dependent on coconut as their major source of income. There is now an opportunity for these people to find employment so that their children don't need to roam the streets looking for food.

I was amazed at how a single book could influence the lives of so many people. This was the answer I was seeking in order to help save millions of children from a life of poverty, sickness, and malnutrition. By stimulating the demand for coconut products these people are able to work and make an honest living. They aren't receiving a handout but an opportunity to work and provide for themselves.

Since then, I have dedicated myself to educating the world about the incredible health benefits of coconut oil and other coconut products. I established The Coconut Research Center (www.coconutresearchcenter.org) to help educate both the medical community and general public with the true facts about coconut products. In so doing, my goal is to not only make known the remarkable health benefits of this tropical fruit but to make it possible for those farmers, laborers, processors, and others working in the coconut industry all over the world to make a living that can support themselves and their families.

### Save the Children

Out of this experience came the Save the Children Campaign. The purpose of this program is to help save children and their families from a life of poverty and starvation. The Save the Children Campaign is not a charity. We don't sell

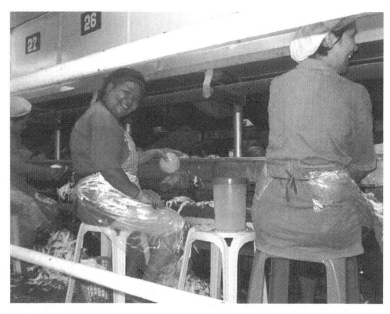

*Workers in a coconut processing facility.*

products or solicit donations. Our approach is to educate. As people learn about the health benefits of coconut products they will begin to use them. When you purchase coconut products you provide a means by which economically disadvantage parents can make a living so that they can feed, cloth, and educate their children. While you are helping others in this manner, you are also improving your own health. It's a win-win situation for everyone involved.

**Major Objectives. of the Save the Children Campaign**

1. Help people achieve better health through the use of coconut products. You, me, and everyone else who uses coconut products can benefit from using this miracle food.

2. Provide a means for employment and economic development, especially in areas where coconuts are an abundant natural resource. Parents are able to earn a living that allows them to provide for the needs of their children. In

many Third World countries coconut palms are an abundant renewable natural resource waiting to be put to use.

3. Reduce the occurrence of malnutrition and birth defects in children. Children who have gone hungry since birth and are malnourished can be fed. Pregnant women can get better nutrition so their babies aren't born with birth defects. Nursing mothers are able to provide their babies breast milk with a higher level of nutrition so their children can grow and develop properly.

4. Provide an affordable alternative to costly drugs, especially in economically disadvantaged areas. For many people, especially in Third World countries, drugs are out of reach because of their cost. Coconut oil and other coconut products, which cost far less, can often be used in place of some drugs. Coconut is considered a functional food, meaning it offers health benefits beyond it nutritional content. Since it is a food it does not have adverse side effects, as do many drugs.

How can you help save the children and accomplish the objectives listed above? It's easy. All you need to do is tell people about the benefits of using coconut products. It's that simple. It doesn't take much effort. Guide them to the Coconut Research Center website (www.coconutresearchcenter.

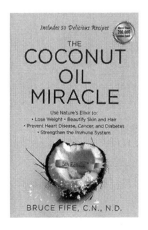

*The book that started it all, now in its 5th edition.*

*Dr. Dilodilo with some of the children in the Philippines who are benefiting from the Save the Children Campaign.*

org) and encourage them to read the book *The Coconut Oil Miracle*. Education is the key. As people learn about the health benefits of coconuts they will start using them. They benefit themselves, the coconut growers and their families and the environment.

**TYPES OF COCONUT OIL**

Coconut oil is extracted from coconut meat. There are many methods in which the oil can be extracted but the end product results in basically one of two types of oil: virgin or non-virgin.

Virgin coconut oil, also referred to as VCO, is produced from fresh coconuts with minimal processing. There are two ways to accomplish this. The first is to shred the coconut and then dry it on a drying rack to reduce the water content. The dried coconut is then placed it in an oil press and the oil is squeeze out. In small scale operations a hand operated hydraulic oil press is usually used. In the second method, fresh coconut is shredded and immediately squeezed to extract the oil and water. In this case, the water needs to be removed. The simplest way to do this is to let the mixture stand for a day or two and allow the oil and water to naturally separate. The oil being lighter than the water will float to the top and can be scooped off. Another method is to put the mixture into a large centrifuge, which will remove the water in just a few minutes. Sometimes the oil is heated slightly after extraction to drive off additional moisture. This generally results in a higher quality oil with a longer shelf life.

Non-virgin coconut oil is generally made from copra—sun dried coconut—and goes through more extensive processing that involves higher temperatures and filtering. Chemical extraction agents are not usually used in coconut oil processing. Refined coconut oil is often referred to as RBD coconut oil, a term that stands for Refined, Bleached, and Deodorized. This is the type of oil typically produced by large scale producers.

Virgin coconut oil is the type of oil typically produced in small or community operations. Because virgin coconut oil has gone through minimal processing it retains its coconut aroma and flavor. The smell and flavor comes primarily from the polyphenols in the oil. In processed coconut oil most of the polyphenols are removed so the oil has no smell or taste. Although polyphenols have some health benefits, they are minor constituents in coconut oil. It is the medium chain fatty acids in the oil that set it apart and give it its distinctive health-promoting properties. These medium chain fatty acids are not removed or altered in processing. Consequently, virgin coconut oil is only slightly better than processed coconut oil in terms of its effects on health.

Nearly all of the studies on the health effects of coconut oil that have established coconut oil as one of the premier health foods, were conducted using processed coconut oil.

So, regardless of the more extensive processing, refined coconut oil is still a very healthy oil. The advantage it has over virgin coconut oil is the lack of the coconut flavor. Many people like it, but there are some who don't like the taste of coconut or like having everything they eat taste like coconut. If you like the taste of coconut oil and want the healthiest oil possible, then virgin coconut oil is the best to use.

When you go to the store it can be confusing as to which products are virgin and which are processed because so many different terms are used such as organic, natural, expeller pressed, etc. There is a simply way to tell the difference. Virgin coconut oils will always have the word "virgin" on the label. Processed coconut oils will not use this term. The label may state they are organic or natural but if the word virgin is not indicated, then it is processed. Processed coconut oil tends to be a little less expensive than virgin coconut oil.

A characteristic of both virgin and processed coconut oil is its high melting point. Coconut oil melts at 76° F (24° C). At temperatures above this the oil is a clear liquid. When the temperature drops below this the oil becomes solid and turns white. The transition between liquid and solid is a natural characteristic of all oils. Olive oil, for example, is liquid at room temperature but place it in the refrigerator and it will turn solid. All oils will do this at some temperature. So don't be surprised if you purchase a bottle of white coconut oil and bring it home and notice that in a few days in a warm kitchen cupboard it has transformed into a clear liquid. This is normal and natural.

# 2

# 1001 Uses for Coconut Oil

It is said that there are a thousand uses for the coconut palm. Asian and Pacific Islanders use it for a multitude of purposes from building materials and clothing to food and medicine. Of all the products from the coconut palm the fruit—the coconut—is the most valuable. From the coconut you can get meat, milk, oil, water, and vinegar. Of these, coconut oil is the most versatile. In fact, it is the most useful and versatile of all the fats and oils.

Coconut oil and its components (fatty acids) are used in cooking and food preparation, infant formulas, enteral (tube feeding) and parenteral (intravenous) nutritional formulas for hospital patients, as carriers for transdermal delivery of medication, anti-fungal, antibacterial, and antiviral medications, skin creams and lotions, sunscreens, cosmetics, toothpastes, soaps and detergents, lubricants, biofuels, and numerous other pharmaceutical and industrial applications. In fact, there are literally thousands of uses for the oil.

In this chapter I have listed many uses for coconut oil. Not all possible uses are included, as new uses are being discovered all the time, particularly in medicine, and there are some uses I am not yet aware of. I've limited entries to documented medical, nutritional, industrial, historical and common uses for coconut oil.

I haven't actually counted every item listed below. The list could easily swell to over 1001 items if every medical application were included. For example, coconut oil possesses anti-inflammatory properties and could be useful in treating hundreds of health conditions associated with inflammation. I've only listed those that have been documented.

## FOOD

Flavoring
Texture
Prevent sticking
Cooking/frying oil
Can use in place of margarine, shortening, and vegetable oils in food preparation
Preservative (prevent oxidation/rancidity and bacterial and fungal contamination)
Extend shelf life of foods
Season cookware
Source of healthy fat
Can help balance essential fatty acid consumption
Egg preserver

**Extend Egg Shelf LIfe**
You can extend the shelf life of fresh eggs by applying a thin coat of coconut oil to the unbroken egg shell. Liquefy the coconut oil (but don't make it hot), dip the egg into the oil or brush on a coat of oil over the egg surface then store in a cool place. The oil creates a seal that keeps oxygen from penetrating into the eggs. Eggs prepared this way are reported to remain edible for about 9 months.

# NUTRITION AND HEALTH

Nutritional supplement

Improve digestive health/function

Improve absorption of nutrients (vitamins, minerals, amino acids, fat soluble phytonutrients)

Prevent vitamin/mineral deficiencies (enhances nutritional value of the foods)

Improve athletic performance (some professional sports teams use coconut oil in training to boost energy levels and performance such as the UKs Bolton Wanderers soccer and the Leicester Tigers rugby squad)

Enhance fetal growth and brain development

Improve lactation and milk quality

Acts as a protective antioxidant

Provide a quick and easy source of nutrition

Prevent/treat malnutrition (better than other oils)

Fortify infant formula

Fortify hospital feeding formulas

Enrich breast milk (nursing mother consumes the oil)

Help to keep blood sugars in balance (good for diabetics)

Moderates glucose release into bloodstream

Improves insulin secretion

Improves insulin sensitivity

Weight management

Reduces steatorrhea (improves fat indigestion)

Helps heal damage caused by celiac disease, improving nutrient absorption

Helps improve absorption of nutrients after partial surgical removal of the stomach or intestine

Used in parenteral nutrition (delivered by IV to prevent muscle breakdown in critically ill patients)

Used in enteral nutrition (nutrients delivered to patients by tube feeding)

Control sugar cravings

Improve body's utilization of EFAs

Quickly and easily absorbed by cells and converted into energy.

Reduces stress on pancreas (coconut oil reduces need for pancreatic enzymes and hormones)

**Miranda Kerr's Beauty Secret—Coconut Oil.**

Victoria Secret model Miranda Kerr claims that coconut oil is one of the secrets to her success. She says it is the key to her clear skin, shiny hair, and trim figure. "I've been drinking it since I was 14 and it's the one thing I can't live without," she says. "I will not go a day without coconut oil. I personally take four teaspoons per day, either on my salads, in my cooking or in my cups of green tea…

Everyone is different, but that is what works for me and I prefer it as a substitute to other oils more readily used in day-to-day food preparation and cooking." In January 2011 she gave birth to her first child. She says coconut oil was instrumental in helping her quickly regain her supermodel figure and was back modeling just a few months after delivery.

## MEDICINE
**Coconut Oil Can Aid in the Following:**
Heart function
Liver function

Gallbladder function
Kidney function
Pancreas function
Intestine function
Brain function
Immune function
Thyroid function
Prostate health
Improve blood circulation
Improves sperm motility and fertility
Reduce inflammation
Protect against cancer
Protect against seizures
Increase HDL cholesterol values (the good cholesterol)
Improve (lower) cholesterol ratio
Improve lipoprotein (a)/Lp(a) levels
Reduce atherosclerosis
Reduce risk of heart attack and stroke
Protect against heart failure
Protect against diabetes
Protect against metabolic syndrome (abdominal obesity, dyslipidemia, hypertension, impaired fasting glucose)
Improve energy
Boost metabolism
Prevent catabolism/breakdown of muscle protein during fasting, dieting, or heavy exercise

**Helps Prevent and Treat Bacterial Infections**
Peptic ulcers
Boils
Staph infections (including MRSA)
Eye infections (conjunctivitis)
Gingivitis and periodontal disease
Dental cavities and periodontal disease
Fistulas

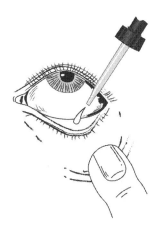

**Treat Minor Eye Conditions**

Coconut oil can be applied directly into the eye to treat infections and wash out dust, irritants and debris. Coconut oil is perfectly safe for use in the eye. It does not sting or hurt. Heat coconut oil until it melts, but is not hot. Tilt your head back or lie down and using an eye dropper put a few drops of the oil in the eye.

Ear infections
Throat infections
Gonorrhea
Toxic shock syndrome
Gastroenteritis
Tetanus
Food poisoning
Sinus infections
Bed sores
Urinary tract infection
Bladder infections
Pneumonia
Rheumatic fever
Meningitis
Anthrax
Parrot fever

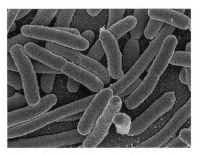

*Coconut oil contains fatty acids that can kill a variety of disease-causing bacteria.*

Spirochetes (Lyme disease, syphilis, etc.)
Gangrene
Endocarditis
Lynphogranuloma venereum
Pelvic inflammatory disease
Mastitis
Swimmer's ear

***Helps Prevent and Treat Fungi/Yeast Infections***
Ringworm
Athlete's foot
Jock Itch
Toenail fungus
Candidiasis
Yeast Infections
Thrush
Diaper rash
Ear fungus/itchy ear

**Helps Prevent and Treat Viral Infections**
Influenza
Intestinal infections/diarrhea
Measles
Herpes (fever blister/cold sore)
Mononucleosis
Hepatitis C
Epstein-Barr
Leukemia virus
Pneumonovirus
Coxsackie virus
Visna virus
Vesicular stomatitis virus
Human lymphotropic virus
Syncytial virus
Sarcoma virus
SARS coronavirus
Parainfluenza virus type 2
AIDS/HIV
Chicken pox
Shingles

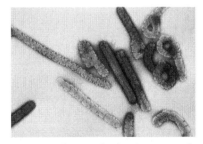

*The medium chain fatty acids in coconut oil kill many disease-causing viruses.*

**Helps Prevent and Treat Parasitic Infections**
Giardia
Protozoa
Lice
Scabies
Intestinal worms (tapeworms, pinworms, etc.)

**Helps Prevent and Treat Neurological Disorders**
Epilepsy
Parkinson's
Dementia (vascular dementia, Lewy Body dementia,
    frontotemporal dementia, etc)
Alzheimer's
Huntington's
Multiple sclerosis (MS)
Amyotrophic Lateral Sclerosis (ALS)
Strokes
Traumatic brain injury
Narcolepsy
Schizophrenia
Insomnia
Autism
ADHD
Down syndrome
Infantile spasms
Migraine headaches
Depression
Brain fog
Hypoxia

*Alzheimer's patients have experienced far better results using coconut oil than any of the medications currently on the market.*

**Speeds Healing from Trauma/Injury**
Shortens recovery time after surgery
Circumcision
Laceration, road rash
Cuts

Burns/sunburns
Bruises
Bee and wasp stings
Spider, sand fly, ant, and other insect bites
Blisters
Poison Ivy or oak
Carpal tunnel syndrome
Acute poisoning (antidote for numerous environmental, industrial, and biological toxins)
Nosebleeds
Sooths and speeds healing of tattoos
Helps stop bleeding
Reduces pain (analgesic)
Reduces fever (antipyretic)
Anti-inflammatory

## Helps Ease Digestive and Malabsorption Disorders
Whipple's disease
Irritable Bowel Syndrome (IBS)
Colitis
Crohn's disease
Muscular carnitine deficiency
Lipoprotein lipase deficiency/Congenital beta-lipoprotein deficiency
Abnormalities of protein metabolism
Malabsorption syndrome
Primary intestinal lymphangiectasia (Waldmann's Disease)
Cholelithiasis (gallstone disease)
Gluten enteropathy
Blind-loop syndrome
Primary biliary cirrhosis
Type V hyperlipoproteinemia
Biliary atresia, obstructive jaundice
Enteritis
Chyluria (milky urine)

Chylothorax
Chylous ascites
Pancreatitis
Hemorrhoids
Pancreatectomy (surgical removal of the pancreas)
Cholecystectomy (surgical removal of the gallbladder)
Balance intestinal flora
Gastrointestnal ulcers

**Useful for the Treatment of Chronic
and Genetic Conditions**
Allergies
Sjogren's syndrome
Prevent/treat neuropathy (restore nerve function)
Prostate enlargement (benign prostatic hyperplasia)
Mast-cell deficiency
Cystic fibrosis
Arthritis
Fibromyalgia
Gout
Asthma
Diabetes
Obesity
Osteoporosis, Osteomalacia, Rickets
Low thyroid function
Hypoglycemia
Rheumatic fever
Altitude sickness
Anemia
Constipation
Hemorrhoids
Chronic fatigue syndrome
Polycystic ovary syndrome
Menstrual irregularities
Retinopathy

Nephropathy
Peripheral vascular disease
Protects the liver from the effects of alcohol and drug abuse and infection
Keratosis pilaris

**Other**
Reduce side effects of conventional cancer treatments (chemotherapy/radiation therapy)
Carrier for medications
Drug preservative
Improve lipid based drug solubility in water
Remove ear wax
Eye wash

## VETERINARY MEDICINE

All the health benefits mentioned for humans also applies to animals. Many pet owners give their pets coconut oil to improve their health. People are using coconut oil to successfully treat animals with a wide variety is health issues such as diabetes, cancer, infections, skin diseases, and more. Some conditions associated with animals include:

Bad breath (doggy breath)
Body odor
Improve shine on coat
Prevent birds from picking skin and feathers
Expel or kill intestinal parasites
Flea, tick, and mite repellent
Clear up hot spots
Use as an udder balm for goats, cows, and other animals

## BODY CARE
Soften and sooth dry, scaly, itchy skin
Emollient

Exfoliant
Prevent wrinkles
Prevent/lighten aging (liver) spots
Makeup remover
Sooth chapped lips
Moisturizer
Deodorant
Eye cream
Protect against UV radiation/sunscreen lotion
Suntan lotion (protects against burning while giving a light
    tan)
Prevent premature aging of skin
Sooth itchy skin
Soften cracked, callused heels
Massage oil
Mouthwash
Toothpaste
Prevent/treat bad breath
Prevent/treat dandruff
Prevent/treat cradle cap
Clear acne
Dissolve and remove ear wax
Remove Warts/moles
Prevent skin infections
Speed healing of wounds
Stop bleeding of wounds
Eases pain and inflammation caused by insect bites
Nipple cream when nursing
Treat diaper rash
Head lice
Hives
Insect repellent
Eczema/psoriasis/dermatitis
Aftershave lotion
Hair conditioner

**Natural Insect Repellent**

Mix 2 tablespoons of coconut oil with 10-25 drops of lemon eucalyptus, regular eucalyptus, or citronella oil. Even if an insect does bite, you won't have a bad reaction because the oil sooths itchiness and irritation from the very start so no welt, blister or redness develops.

Hair styling agent (apply a small amount to hair for a healthy, glossy look)
Dental care/toothpaste/mouthwash
Deodorant
Massage oil
Personal Lubricant
Stretch mark cream
Scare remover
Skin conditioner—balances skin pH, apply after bathing
Genital warts

**Scar Remover**

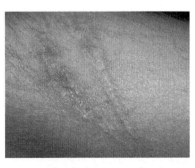

About 15 years ago I was helping a friend load a moving truck. While lifting a metal bed frame up onto to truck, part of the frame slipped, fell, and hit me in the forehead. It bled profusely and left a noticeable inch-long scar. I had this scar for many years but never paid much attention to it because there was nothing I could do about it. Some years later I started using coconut oil in my hair fairly regularly. After several months I realized the scare was no longer visible. It must have been the coconut oil because I had the scar for many years and then almost suddenly it was gone.

## INDUSTRIAL

Soap (highest quality, naturally disinfectant, antimicrobial, lathers up even in salt water)
Shampoo
Biofuel/biodiesel
Jet fuel
Lamp fuel
Engine lubricant/motor oil
Hydraulic press fluid
Leather softener
Condition wood cutting boards
Wood polish

**Washing Greasy Hands**

Grease and oil from engines and machinery are difficult to wash off the hands using ordinary soap and water. Hardcore soaps like Lava remove part of your skin along with the grease or contain toxic solvents that are absorbed into your skin. There is a better, healthier solution—coconut oil. Coconut oil cuts through the grease, loosening and dissolving it so that most of it can be wiped off with a paper towel. Wash hands as usual with regular soap and water to remove the excess oil and remaining softened grease.

Bronze polish

Lubricant (hinges, machinery, etc.)

Degreasing agent for machinery

Rust inhibitor

Hand degreaser

Dissolve grease under fingernails

Chewing gum remover (can dissolve gum stuck in hair, carpet, clothing, or shoe)

Useful in removing makeup and lipstick from clothing and carpeting

Detergent

Remove labels from bottles (acts and an adhesive solvent)

Environmentally friendly fabrication of silver and gold nanoparticles for use in nanotechnology

Provides basic material for making oleochemicals for manufacturer of hundreds of products such as detergents, solvents, plastics, grease, resins, lubricants, etc.)


**COCONUT OIL TOOTHPASTE ANYONE?**

Eating too many candy bars and gummy bears might send you to the dentist. But adding coconut into your diet may save you that dreaded trip. Could coconut be the next miracle ingredient toothpaste manufacturers start putting into their products? Many people already brush their teeth with coconut oil to take advantage of its germ-fighting, anti-cavity effects. A recent study adds more evidence to coconut oil's ability to ward of tooth decay.[1]

Tooth decay, or dental caries is an infection that causes the breakdown and eventual destruction of the organic matter of the tooth, and is the most common disease in the world. New research from the Athlone Institute of Technology in Ireland shows that the unique fatty acids found in coconut oil are able to attack bacteria that cause tooth decay.

The research team tested the antibacterial action of coconut oil in two states. In its natural state, and in a second state where they treated the coconut oil with enzymes to simulate a process similar to digestion, thus breaking down the oil into individual fatty acids. The oils were then tested against strains of Streptococcus bacteria, common inhabitants of the mouth. What they discovered was that the enzyme-modified coconut oil (medium chain fatty acids) strongly inhibited the growth of most strains of Streptococcus bacteria including *Streptococcus mutans*—an acid-producing bacterium that is the primary causative agent in the formation of dental caries in humans.

"Dental caries is a commonly overlooked health problem affecting 60-90 percent of children and the majority of adults in industrialized countries," says Dr Damien Brady who is leading the research. "Incorporating enzyme-modified coconut oil (MCFAs) into dental hygiene products would be an attractive alternative to chemical additives, particularly as it works at relatively low concentrations. Also, with increasing antibiotic resistance, it is important that we turn our attention to new ways to combat microbial infection."

This study, however, is just the first step. The research group will further their study to examine how coconut oil interacts with Streptococcus bacteria at the molecular level and discover which other strains of harmful bacteria and yeasts it is active against. Further testing by the group at the Athlone Institute of Technology found that enzyme-modified coconut oil was also harmful to the yeast *Candida albicans* that can cause thrush a common oral yeast infection.

For now the researchers suggest that enzyme-modified coconut oil (MCFAs) has potential as a marketable antimicrobial that could be of particular interest to the oral healthcare industry.

This study is really nothing new. Studies published 40 years ago showed the same results. However, back then it didn't generate as much interest as it is today. A number of scientists are now taking notice of the remarkable potential of coconut oil and perusing useful studies with it. It seems that a new generation of scientists, who are more open-minded, are rediscovering the remarkable benefits of coconut oil. It is a shame that the anti-fat, anti-saturated fat mindset that prevailed in medicine over the past several decades caused scientists and doctors to ignore previous studies like these for so long.

## MAN SURVIVES 30 YEARS ON COCONUTS AND RAIN WATER

Coconuts are highly nutritious. In fact, they provide enough nutrition that you could live entirely on them and nothing else. There are numerous accounts of people who have been stranded on tropical islands who have managed to survive weeks and even months living on little more than coconuts. How long can a person live with coconut being the only nourishment? There are no studies but it appears a person can live a long time—decades—on nothing more than coconuts and water.[2]

Mark Cola is a living example, for the past 30 years his diet has consisted entirely of dried coconut and rainwater. Cola lives on Icacos—a small uninhabited island off the coast of Puerto Rico. The island is a popular snorkeling and tourist destination. No one lives there. There are no facilities. Villagers who live in the nearby fishing community marvel at Cola's primitive survival techniques, repetitious meals, and his isolation from society.

Describing Cola as a hermit, villagers say they have never seen him visit a supermarket, bar, restaurant or clothing store in the three decades he has been residing on the beach. Neither does he socialize nor engage in conversations with anyone. He goes months at a time without speaking with anyone. Cola loves his secluded lifestyle.

*The island of Icacos.*

At one time, Cola lived a normal life with his family in the nearby community. One day as a youth he went on a deep-sea trawler and jumped overboard. He swam to shore and never went back home. No one knows why and he has never told anyone why he chose to live outdoors.

His "home" is located several meters from the shoreline. At times, Cola takes a bath in the sea, but hardly ventures away from the beach.

Cola has been observed practicing Chinese martial arts. A small punching bag, which hangs from a makeshift goalpost is used by Cola to keep fit. His surroundings are immaculate.

Cola sleeps under a makeshift structure—a concrete slab and stones less than two feet high, supports five sheets of galvanized metal. Rocks were strategically placed on top of the metal sheets to keep them from blowing away. To sleep at night, Cola crawls under the metal sheets. The sheets, which are built on a slant, serve as a catchment for rainwater, which Cola collects in plastic containers and buckets.

This water is then used for drinking, bathing, and washing his few pieces of clothing. Above his living quarters, a massive sea grape tree sways in the breeze. Cola clads himself with garments left behind by sea bathers or visitors. He wears whatever clothing he finds on the beach, including female clothing and underwear. A pile of coconuts sits near a table made from tree branches. On the table sits a grater to shred coconut.

Cola makes his own coconut oil by squeezing the milk from grated coconut. He combines the milk with a little water and allows it to ferment. The oil collects on the surface of the mixture where it is easy to scoop up. The oil is used on his flawless skin and hair, which glistens under the blistering sun.

Coconuts, Cola said, have been his main staple for years. "It's all that I eat. There are no fruit trees around. I don't hunt animals or fish. I enjoy what nature has to offer."

Mark Cola wearing women's underwear, poses for photo on the beach. Photo: Abraham Diaz.

# COCONUT OIL FOR BRAIN HEALTH

Alzheimer's is a dreaded disease. Few other diseases can elicit the fear and sense of hopelessness that comes with a diagnosis of Alzheimer's. The gradual decline in mental function often begins with barely noticeable lapses in memory followed by losses in the ability to plan and execute familiar tasks, and to reason and execute judgment. Eventually, memory loss increases in severity until it is incapacitating. The ability to articulate words correctly and changes in mood and personality may also be evident. Emotional problems such as easy agitation, poor judgment, mental confusion, feelings of withdrawal, disorientation, and hallucinations are common. Affected individuals may also develop seizures and incontinence, requiring constant attention and care. Death is the final outcome. Alzheimer's is the seventh leading cause of death in the United States.

Alzheimer's usually surfaces sometime after the age of 60. The disease affects 1 in 8 people over the age of 65 and affects nearly half of those over 85. In a small number of people it occurs in their 40s or 50s.

The incidence of Alzheimer's is growing rapidly. In 1979 the disease affected only about 0.2 people out of every 100,000. By 2006 that number shot up to 20 per 100,000. Incidence is expected to double over the next 20 years.

Currently there is no effective medical treatment for the disease. A diagnosis of Alzheimer's is essentially a death sentence. Treatment focuses on reducing the severity of the symptoms, combined with providing services and support to make living with the disease more manageable. Patients must endure the disease through all stages of degeneration until the bitter end.

Fortunately, however, there is a way to both prevent and reverse Alzheimer's. It doesn't require drugs, surgeries, radiation, high tech medical devices, or psychiatric treatment. The solution is in the diet.

The fundamental problem associated with Alzheimer's disease is the inability of the brain to effectively utilize glucose, or blood sugar, to produce energy. As a result, the brain rapidly ages and degenerates into dementia.

In addition to glucose, the brain can also use ketones to produce energy. The advantage of ketones is that they can bypass the defects in glucose energy metabolism associated with Alzheimer's. Therefore, if enough ketones are available on a continual basis, they could satisfy the brain's energy needs.

Fortunately there are certain dietary fats, namely medium chain triglycerides (MCTs), that are readily converted into ketones in the body. The addition of MCTs into the diet can produce very positive effects on the brain, providing a new tool with which to fight Alzheimer's. In clinical studies MCTs have produced better results in Alzheimer's patients than any other treatment currently known.

In one study for instance, Alzheimer's patients consumed a beverage containing MCTs or a beverage without MCTs. Those who drank the beverage containing the MCTs had markedly increased blood ketone levels after 90 minutes when a cognitive test was administered. These patients scored significantly better on the test than those who had not consumed the MCTs.[3]

This study was remarkable for the reason that it produced improvement in cogitative function after a single dose of MCTs. No Alzheimer's drug or treatment has ever come close to achieving results like this. Based on studies such as this, a new drug consisting of only MCTs has been approved by the FDA for the treatment of Alzheimer's disease.

MCT-based drugs aren't really necessary. They are expensive and require a prescription. Any source of MCTs can work just as well. The normal way we get MCTs is in our diet. However, there are few good natural dietary sources of MCTs. By far the largest natural source of MCTs is found in coconut oil. Coconut oil is composed predominately of MCTs, amounting to about 63 percent of the total. The MCTs used in Alzheimer's studies and to produce pharmaceuticals comes from coconut oil. The amount of MCTs in coconut oil is great enough to produce therapeutic blood levels of ketones. Two tablespoons of coconut oil can produce enough ketones to have a significant effect on brain function and can be used for the treatment of Alzheimer's.

Mary Newport, MD proved that coconut oil alone or in combination with MCT oil can effectively stop the progression of Alzheimer's disease and reverse the symptoms. Her husband Steve, suffered from the disease for nearly six years before he began taking coconut oil. The results were immediate and dramatic.

Prior to taking coconut oil he was diagnosed with moderately severe Alzheimer's. He could no longer take care of himself. He required supervision to complete many day-to-day tasks such as replacing a light bulb, vacuuming, doing a load of laundry, washing dishes, and dressing appropriately. He was easily distracted when attempting such tasks, and never got around to completing them. He was no longer able to use a computer keyboard or calculate or perform basic arithmetic. He was unable to read because words seemed to move about the page erratically, he had difficulty spelling simple words, such as "out" and "put" and had trouble recalling many common words when speaking. He had physical difficulties as well, including a moderate hand tremor that interfered with eating and a jaw tremor that was most apparent while speaking. He walked slowly with an abnormal gait which involved pulling each foot up higher than usual with each step. An MRI showed significant loss of brain mass particularly in the areas involved in memory and cognitive abilities. Drugs such as Aricept, Namenda, and Exelon proved to be of no help.

After taking coconut oil, his scores on Alzheimer's rating scales improved dramatically. Within just a couple of weeks his score on the Mini Mental Status Exam, a standard test for Alzheimer's, went from a low of 12 out of 30 to 18. A very significant improvement, which is unheard of since Alzheimer's is a progressive disease that doesn't get better over time. It always gets worse. His score continued to improve, elevating him from moderately severe up to a mild stage of Alzheimer's.

His memory has improved dramatically. He can recall events that happened days or weeks earlier and relays telephone conversations accurately. He is more focused when performing tasks and is able to complete household and gardening chores with minimal to no supervision. His ability to initiate and continue a conversation has improved and his sense of humor has returned. He has regained his ability to read and the ability to type. His facial tremor is gone with minimal to no hand tremor. He walks with a normal gait and can run for the first time in more than a year.

He has improved so significantly that he began volunteering twice a week at the hospital where his wife works, helping in the warehouse and delivering supplies. He is pleased with his job and enjoys the people with whom he works. He continues to improve. With a smile on his face he exclaims "I've got my life back." Other Alzheimer's patients who are incorporating coconut oil into their diets are experiencing similar results.

Researchers suggest that raising blood ketone levels by consuming coconut oil or by other means is the most promising form of treatment for not only Alzheimer's but for a number of neurodegenerative disorders including Parkinson's disease, epilepsy, amyotrophic lateral sclerosis (ALS), Huntington's disease, and multiple sclerosis. Who could have imagined that a simple dietary intervention could have such a remarkable effect on brain health?

## ANIMALS BENEFIT FROM COCONUT OIL

Coconut, and especially coconut oil, is gaining a reputation as a health food and natural healer. People are using it to improve digestion, clear up skin problems, boost energy levels, aid in weight loss, fight off infections, balance blood sugar, and bring improvement to numerous other conditions (see *Coconut Cures: Preventing and Treating Common Health Problems with Coconut,* www.piccadillybooks.com).

Having written several books on the health aspects of coconut, I am often asked if it can be of benefit to animals as well. My answer is a most definite "Yes!" Most pets love the taste of coconut oil and will readily eat it. Virtually every health benefit associated with coconut oil in humans is applicable to animals. In fact, much of what we know about the health aspects of coconut oil was first observed in animals.

Like it or not, scientists often use animals in their research. For instance, we know of coconut oil's anticancer properties because when researchers feed it to lab animals or apply it on their skin, they don't get cancer. We know that coconut oil neutralizes a variety of toxins because animals are protected from these poisons if given the oil. Animal studies also demonstrate how and why coconut oil digests easier than other oils and how it is converted into energy rather than body fat, which increases energy, and stimulates metabolism. The antiviral, antibacterial, and antifungal effects of coconut oil have been demonstrated in animals. These studies have also shown that coconut oil is well tolerated, causing the animals no harm, unlike many drugs and other treatments.

So it makes sense that coconut oil can be of great benefit to pet owners. Pets, like humans, suffer from a variety of health problems. Coconut oil offers a simple, inexpensive, and easy remedy to many of these problems. Over the years I've heard numerous testimonies from pet owners describing how coconut oil, as well as coconut meat, has been helpful. Coconut oil has shown to be of benefit to all types of animals including dogs, cats, and birds, as well as horses, cows, goats,

and other farm animals. Some of the benefits owners have reported include: reduced or elimination of body odor and bad breath; healthier skin and elimination of rashes, itchiness, etc.; coats becoming shinny and healthy looking; improved energy; better digestion; reduction in excess weight; relief from arthritic-like symptoms; cleared-up infections; expulsion of worms; and improved over-all health. Applied topically it aids in the healing of cuts, bites, stings, and infections. There have also been some reports of healing from very serious conditions such as poisoning, cancer, and diabetes.

It sounds remarkable and maybe even unbelievable, but you don't need to take my word for it. You can read for yourself what pet owners are saying. Let me share with you a few of the testimonies. Here you can see for yourself what pet owners are experiencing with coconut oil.

Coconut oil has long been known for it healing effect on the skin when applied topically. Dry, rough, itchy skin becomes smooth and soft within a matter of days. Infections, warts, wounds, and such heal remarkable well with the daily application of coconut oil as the following describe. The most common type of coconut oil used by pet owners is virgin coconut oil (VCO).

"My dog Katie had a tiny pink lump on her chin. It gradually grew larger so we brought her to the vet, who diagnosed it as folliculitis (a skin infection surrounding hair follicles). He said to wait until it got bigger and he would do surgery to remove it. It grew to the size of a pea and became a very angry reddish pink in color. It was really terrible to look at and right on her pretty face! I didn't want to put her through the surgery so I decided to try coconut oil after reading about other's success with skin problems.

"I applied coconut oil daily. Gradually the lump reduced in size and the color became normal. After about two weeks I noticed it had broken and become crusty. I kept applying the oil daily and now a month later it is very tiny and a normal skin color. I really had to look to find it! I'm really happy with the coconut oil."

Bernadette

"I have a 14 year old Lhaso. For about two years now, she's had a scabby rash and all she did was lick it and itch 24-7. I was at my wits end with her, as I tried everything and she still itched. Well, this time last week I thought, what the heck if it's good for people then it'll be good for my dog Candy. So I put it in her food daily and rubbed it on that spot. It is totally unbelievable but Candy isn't itching and the spot seems to be going away."

P.S.

"I have been feeding coconut oil to my husband's red tabby, Pumpkin. He was climbing into my lap at the table trying to steal it away, so I started putting half a teaspoon in his dinner. I have gradually increased the amount to 1 teaspoon. Almost immediately, we noticed a difference in odor—his cat box used to smell awful whenever he used it, and now there's no odor at all. His breath has improved as well."

C.J

"My nine year old Shar Pei senior dog, suffered from severe arthritis with bad hips and almost non-existent front elbows. The vets suggested I put him to sleep for he needed both front and rear wheels to stay mobile. Being an individual that doesn't take 'impossible' for an answer, I did my own research...After only two weeks of organic extra virgin coconut oil with one tablespoon per 50 pounds, Taz was up and running like a puppy on all four legs. After putting one tablespoon of organic virgin coconut oil in the dog's food daily, Taz was better. It has been over a year, and he's still truckin'."

Beverly

My neighbor has a female Doberman that they adore. She became very ill and could not stand. Their vet said Dobermans often develop "wobblers" and there was not much they could do. It was degenerative and she may have about a month to live. They were, of course, crushed. I, of course, never gave up and told him to add virgin coconut oil to her food. I sent my neighbor home with a small jar of the precious oil. He was willing to try anything. They were having to force feed her a liquid diet at the time. In 24 hours the dog was up! Over the course of the week she continued to improve. He now puts it in her food daily. She no longer wobbles when she walks and all is right with the world! My neighbor was amazed."

S.F.

If you love animals you should be giving them coconut oil. Many veterinarians are now recommending it as a safer and cheaper option to medications. Coconut oil has been so helpful, especially to older animals, that some pet food companies are now adding it to their products. You can read about this and how coconut oil is improving the life of many pets in my book *Coconut Therapy for Pets*.

# 3

# A Sustainable Natural Resource

**GENETICALLY ENGINEERED FOODS**

When you purchase food at the store or restaurant you never know how or where it was produced. The salmon steak you ate for dinner last night may have come from a farm where the fish were raised on genetically engineered (GE) soy meal, or even worse the fish itself may have been genetically engineered—a product of modern science. Salmon is the first of possibly many new genetically modified animals approved for human consumption by The United States Food and Drug Administration (FDA). The genetically altered salmon are engineered to produce a higher level of growth hormone, causing them to reach market size in just half the time as conventionally raised salmon.

Korean scientists have developed hogs with extraordinarily large backsides, the part that pork-eaters particularly value. These grotesque-looking hogs resemble something you might imagine from creepy offspring of animals exposed to high levels of radiation more than they do potential sources of food for human consumption. Their appearance is enough to turn anybody's stomach.

*GE salmon have genes from a Chinook salmon and an ocean pout—a type of ell—that make more than the usual dose of growth hormone, so they reach market size in half the time as natural salmon. A genetically engineered salmon from AquaBounty Technologies, rear, with a conventionally raised sibling roughly the same age.*

Developing animals that produce a greater percentage of prime cuts of meat is a major goal of genetic scientists. However, not all of the genetic manipulations are focused on producing larger animals or animals with grossly expanded body parts. Some animals are developed to enhance or remove certain characteristics. Researchers in Minnesota are developing milk and beef cattle that have no horns. Ranchers typically de-horn cattle when they are calves to make them less likely to inure other animals or the people who handle them. One drawback so far with hornless dairy cows is it that they don't produce any milk, just another glitch to be worked out with further genetic manipulations. In New Zealand scientists have engineered cows that produce milk without the proteins that trigger milk allergies; now everyone can enjoy GE milk.

Even insects are being genetically manipulated. Genetically altered mosquitoes have been developed in an attempt to reduce the risk of dengue fever. There is no guarantee that this experiment will work. Introducing species of animals and insects from one part of the world into other areas to control pests has generally ended up as environmental disasters. A genetically altered insect is foreign to the entire world so there is no telling what might happen.

Farmers have been using GE crops since the 1990s. Currently as much as 80 percent of the foods in the typical American grocery store contain GE ingredients. Proponents of GE foods claim that they are the wave of the future and will increase crop yields and provide a means to feed a growing world population and thus end world hunger. A noble cause indeed, but is it true? Will converting conventional crops to GE varieties end world hunger? Will it even increase crop yields? Or, as some critics claim, will it be a colossal failure or even worse, usher in an environmental catastrophe and economic disaster?

We hear a lot about the potential harm caused by consuming gluten, sugar, artificial sweeteners, trans fats, preservatives, and such. Of all the ingredients in our foods, what ones are potentially the most troubling? While all of those mentioned have their issues, potentially the most troubling foods are those that contain GE or genetically modified (GM) ingredients. Not only do they pose a threat to our health, but they are dangerous to the environment. What makes them especially troubling is the fact that in places like the US, there are no labeling laws to inform you which foods contain GE ingredients.

The biotech firms that produce GE seeds, the Grocery Manufacturers Association (a consortium of food producers and manufactures) and their friends in government are continually telling us that GE foods are completely safe and there is no need to worry. Thus, causing many people to be in a state of ignorance about the real dangers of these foods.

Awareness about the potential risks of genetically engineered foods is growing. This is due largely because of the publicity generated by individual states that have put to vote whether or not to require foods that contain GE ingredients be identified on the label. Giant corporations and their associates like Monsanto (and other biotech companies) and the Grocery Manufacturers Association have been fighting bitterly to prevent consumers from knowing what's in their foods. The latest polls suggest more than 90 percent of Americans now want to know what's in their foods (according to a poll conducted by MSNBC).

A number of scientists have raised warnings about the danger of GE foods. The evidence is strong enough to convince many governments to ban them or at least establish labeling laws so their citizens know what they are buying. Currently 64 nations require the labeling of foods containing GE ingredients including Austria, Germany, Switzerland, Italy, New Zealand, Australia, Greece, Poland, Malaysia, Brazil, Russia, India, and even China.

Most Americans are totally unaware that they are already eating GE foods. There are no labeling laws at present to inform them. Since the 1990s GE foods have slowly and quietly filtered into our food system. Today, approximately 80 percent of the foods sold in stores and restaurants contain at least some GE ingredients.

About 90 percent of all corn, soybeans, rapeseed/canola, sugar beets, and cotton grown in the US are genetically altered. If you eat anything that contains these foods you are most likely eating GE products. You say you don't eat corn or soy. Think again. Corn is in almost everything. Corn is used in corn meal and flour, oil, and high fructose corn syrup. How many products are cooked in corn oil or contain high fructose corn syrup? Lots! Most foods now are sweetened with high fructose corn syrup—cakes, cookies, ice cream, candy, ketchup, salad dressing, bread,…the list can go on and on. Likewise with soy. Soybean oil is found everywhere. It is one of the most common cooking oils, especially hydrogenated soybean oil which is used extensively in restaurants and for all types of prepared foods. Like corn, soy in one form or another is found in thousands of consumer products. Canola oil is also widely used in food production and restaurants. With the awareness of the dangers of trans fats from hydrogenated oils, many food producers are turning to canola oil instead. Look at the multitude of the foods that contain sugar. The source of that sugar is most likely GE sugar beets. What about cotton? We don't eat that right? Wrong! Cottonseed oil is a major source of hydrogenated oil used in the food industry. All of these GE crops are also used to feed livestock. The chicken, beef, pork, and even fish we buy at the store are often raised on GE crops. In addition, we are also exposed to GE wheat, squash, papaya, and other foods.

## GENETIC ENGINEERING IS AN IMPRECISE SCIENCE

Trying to control genetic changes through artificial modification is a dangerous game. It is dangerous because it enables genes to be transferred between species that would never be possible otherwise. Genetic modification involves injecting a gene from one species of plant or animal into a completely different and naturally incompatible species, yielding unexpected and often unpredictable results.

Much of the genetic research that is going on is hidden from the public because biotech firms require their employees sign legally binding secrecy agreements that forbid them from talking about their research with anyone.

According to geneticist Dr Jonathan Latham, who published an independent study on GE plants, genetic engineering is very imprecise and is making a mess of plant genomes. The process causes unexpected gene mutations and DNA damage. Most GE plants contain more than one genetic modification, some of the plants his team evaluated had as many as 40 different foreign genes in them.[1] Latham says that some of the gene combinations in commercially available plants are so complex that even the biotech companies have given up on trying to assess the potential damage done to the plant's DNA. In other words, even the scientists don't know what they are creating, let alone what effect they will have on our health and the environment.

The insertion of plant, animal, bacterial, and viral genes in food crops can lead to unpredictable and uncontrollable results. Examples of unforeseen changes witnessed in GE foods include poor crop performance, altered nutritional content, increased levels of toxins and allergens in foods, and potential harm to the environment and ecosystems.

Genetic engineering of food crops are designed specifically to be resistant to herbicides (such as Monsanto's weed killer Roundup), be resistant to certain pests, or to produce their own insecticide to discourage insect damage. Herbicide resistant crops can withstand exposure to huge doses of chemical weed killers without harm, while indigenous plants nearby wither and die. Plants designed to produce their own toxic chemicals supplement chemical sprays to keep insects at bay. GE crops can contain multiple genetic alternations so that they are resistant to several types of herbicides and produce their own insecticides. Sounds appetizing doesn't it?

As of yet, GE crops are not designed to produce larger plants or be more productive. It's all about managing pests.


## DIFFERENCES IN GE AND NON-GE PLANTS

Biotech companies claim that GE crops are no different from conventional crops in nutritional quality and safety.

The claim that GE foods are materially comparable to conventional foods, and therefore inherently safe, is false when you consider GE crops are designed to be different. A recent study published in the journal *Food Chemistry* reveals that there are distinct differences.[2] The researchers analyzed soybeans produced under three separate conditions: (1) genetically modified, glyphosate-tolerant soy, (2) unmodified soy cultivated using a conventional chemical cultivation regime, and (3) unmodified soy produced using an organic cultivation regime.

The researchers stated, "Using 35 different nutritional and elemental variables to characterize each soy sample, we were able to discriminate GM, conventional, and organic soybeans *without exception*, demonstrating *substantial nonequivalence* in compositional characteristics for ready-to-market soybeans." GE soybeans actually had a reduced level of important nutrients and therefore, were less nutritious than conventional soybeans.

Roundup Ready cops are engineered to withstand exposure to massive doses that would normally kill the plant as well as all surrounding weeds. As a consequence, GE crops are heavily sprayed, much more so than conventional crops. Even if the nutritional levels were the same, the high level of spraying makes the GE crops less healthful simply because they contain a much higher level of herbicide residue.

Plants that are sprayed with herbicides and insecticides can be taken home and washed or peeled to make them safer because most of the chemical residue clings to the surface of the food.

However, with GE plants, you can't wash out the insecticides that have been placed there genetically because it is in every cell of the plant. It is in what you eat.

Over 37 percent of the GE crops have stacked genes.— two or more GE genes inserted into them. So the plant is not just resistance to Roundup but to other herbicides and may also contain genes to produce their own insecticides. These are the types of GE foods we and the animals in our food supply are being fed.


## ENVIRONMENTAL EFFECT

One of the purposes of GE crops is so that more herbicides can be sprayed on them to annihilate all other plants. Herbicides are designed to kill native plants. Tons of herbicides and insecticides are sprayed on farms around the world. Winds, water, rain, and insects spread them throughout the environment, into the soil and water wreaking havoc wherever they go—it doesn't take a genius to see the tremendous damage these poisons pose to the environment.

With the advent of Roundup Ready crops, use of glyphosate (the active ingredient in Roundup) has significantly risen with about 1 billion pounds sprayed on crops every year. That's 1 billion pounds of herbicide released into the environment annually just from this one product.

Glyphosate's toxicity is well established, with adverse health effects ranging from birth defects to endocrine dysfunction to cancer.[3] Glyphosate is classified as a Class 2A "probable human carcinogen" by the International Agency for Research on Cancer (IARC), a division of the World Health Organization (WHO).

Unbelievably, the US Department of Agriculture (USDA) admits foods are not tested for glyphosate residues due to the high cost of doing such tests. GE crops are heavily contaminated with glyphosate, much more so than conventional crops; this fact alone blows a massive hole in the safety claim.

The increased use of Roundup has caused glyphosate–resistant super weeds to proliferate, leading to a greater use of the herbicides and greater harm to the environment. Current GE crops are being replaced with new varieties that can withstand even heavier doses of herbicides.

*Monsanto's Lasso herbicide to be sprayed on food crops.*

Despite the mounting evidence questioning glyphosate's safety, the Environmental Protection Agency (EPA) raised the allowable limits of glyphosate in our food and feed crops. Allowable levels in oilseed crops, such as soy and canola, have been doubled from 20 ppm to 40 ppm. Permissible glyphosate levels in many other foods have been raised by 15 to 25 times previous levels. Root and tuber vegetables got one of the largest boosts, with allowable residue limits being raised form 0.2 ppm to 6.0 ppm. Crops fed to livestock can have much higher levels, up to 400 ppm or more. All GE crops have glyphosate residue. When you eat GE foods, you really can't divorce the fact that you're also eating glyphosate.

Pesticides and herbicides kill more than just noxious pests, they destroy wildlife that is essential for a healthy environment and food supply. For example, with the increased use of GE crops and massive spraying, Monarch butterfly and honey bee populations have been decimated in the US. It has been estimated that in some areas of the country there has been an 80 percent decline in these important insects within the past few years. This might not sound too alarming, until you consider the impact the absence of just these two insects can have on our lives. Monarch butterflies are pollinators, which makes them important for plant reproduction. They also provide an essential food source for small birds and other animals, which feed larger birds and animals. Monarchs play an important role in ecosystem health and biodiversity. Honey bees too, are pollinators, very important pollinators. Bees are essential for the pollination of numerous flowering plants and food crops. Without them we would lose at least one-third of all our fruits, nuts, and vegetables. It's not just Monarchs and bees that are adversely affected by chemical sprays, but literally millions of insects, animals, and plants as well as humans are harmed by them.

Nearly one billion pounds of Roundup herbicide is used each year for conventional crop production. Genetically

*A self-propelled crop sprayer spraying pesticide on a field.*

engineered crops are more heavily sprayed, since the so-called Roundup Ready crops are designed to withstand lethal doses of this chemical, thus increasing the potential harm to the environment. And that is not to mention all of the other herbicides and pesticides that are also used in agriculture.

Soil is the living skin of the earth. Soil is a combination of granulated rock, water, organic matter, and microbes—bacteria, protozoa, fungi, nematodes, and arthropods. One tablespoon of soil contains about 50 billion living organisms. These microorganisms are key in making nutrients available to plants. The nitrogen, potassium, phosphate, calcium, magnesium, and other essential elements are released into the soil by the activity of microorganisms on rocks and organic matter in the soil. Without this great diversity of living creatures in the soil, plants could not exist. Soil organisms are vital to plant health.

Part of what makes fruits and vegetables good for us are the phytonutrients—plant derived nutrients that help protect us from high blood pressure, glaucoma, cancer, premature aging, and other health problems. Phytonutrients are part of the plant's immune system. Organisms in the soil that we might think of as pests actually stimulate plants to make more phytonutrients. So these small stressors actually, in a sense, enhance our health. Being exposed to different organisms improves the health of the plant and improves our health as well.

Pesticides and other agrichemicals not only kill insects but also the beneficial soil microorganisms, degrading soil quality and fertility. This creates a need to used chemical fertilizers, which can cause more harm by further altering the normal soil ecology, making plants more susceptible to disease and pests. This in turn, prompts the use of more agrichemicals and the further reduction of soil productivity, which encourages the use of more chemical fertilizers. The cycle continues, making the soils less and less productive.

Genetic engineering affects livestock as well. GE plants contain their own insecticides to discourage insects and animals from eating them. Farm animals don't like them either and won't touch them if given the choice. Livestock won't eat them unless they are forced to. When GE feed is all that is available, livestock learn to tolerate it or starve. This is just another form of animal cruelty.

When GE crops are planted, there is nothing to prevent the seeds and pollen from being washed or blown to neighboring farms where they can contaminate non-GE crops. What will happen if they cross bread with native plants? Will the GE gene be passed on? Will heavy spraying cause genetic adaptations in native plants and animals? This has already resulted in the creation of super weeds and super bugs that can withstand pesticide sprays. What will be next?


## WILL NOT ELIMINATE HUNGER

The number one argument and justification for GE crops is the claim that they are needed to prevent starvation and feed the billions of people in the world. Proponents claim GE foods are necessary to feed the world's starving children. Who wouldn't want to do that, right? It's enough to make you want to cry, not because the biotech firms are so benevolent, but because there are people who actually believe this pile of baloney. The one and only reason for GE foods is for profit, pure and simple. There is no intrinsic desire to feed starving people. Their blatant disregard for the health and welfare of people, animals, and the environment is obvious in their refusal to do proper safety and environmental studies and their opposition to independent researchers to do such studies. It is also evident in their fierce opposition to labeling of food and their aggressive persecution of farmers who save GE seeds, as they must purchase new seeds annually or face a lawsuit for patent infringement.

The claim that GE crops will eliminate world hunger conveys the idea that they produce a higher yield than conventional crops. However, this is not true. There is no gene in the plants to make them more productive and they are no better than conventional crops at tolerating poor soils or unstable climate conditions. The claim is based solely on the assumption that yields will be better because GE crops are more resistance to herbicides and to bugs eating them.

GE crops have been around for two decades now, if they are going to save the world from starvation, we would already have seen some evidence of that by now, but we haven't. Pesticides that are required on GE crops poison the soil, kill wildlife, and wreak havoc on the ecosystem contributing to the gradual destruction and loss of productive farmland. This would be a disaster if GE crops were grown around the world.

Most people worldwide simply don't want to eat genetically altered foods. As a result, US exports of soy and corn have declined by as much as $300 million per year just from the lost to European exports alone. Corn exports to China dropped 85 percent from 2013 to 1014. How can GE foods feed the world if the world doesn't want to eat them?


## NOT PROVEN SAFE

Genetic modification of foods has never proven to be safe for humans or the environment. Assessments on safety come only from the biotech corporations themselves, the same companies that profit from these positive safety studies.

Safety studies performed on GE crops fed to animals have generally looked at things such as milk production and meat yield, outcomes that are not relevant to human health. These studies generally do not examine tissues or organs in the animals or look at the biochemistry to identify disease or abnormalities. They are production studies. The vast majority of studies are done to reassure the producers that GE fed animals will live long enough to produce a good yield when they are mature enough to take to market.

There have been very few published studies actually using GE feed. Instead of feeding the test animals GE feed, they just give them the particular proteins the altered plants are suppose to produce. These studies are done using rats. The number of rats used in the studies are too few to produce any real statistically meaningful data. They'll usually observe the rats for only 7 to 14 days, and rarely up to 3 months, and see if the rats die. If they don't, then the GE food containing the protein is declared safe for human consumption regardless of how long or how much a human might consume. We are expected to eat these foods for years, for our entire lives, not just a few days or weeks. However, these proteins, which may come for plants, bacteria, viruses, or animals, can have unknown effects when injected into an entirely a different species. There are no long term studies that actually test GE foods. These so-called "safety" studies are used to justify the claim that GE foods are safe for us to eat for an entire lifetime, from birth to death. No additional studies are needed and, therefore, independent researchers need not bother attempting such studies. Consequently, GE seeds are off limits to them. Outside researchers can't even repeat these studies to verify the results.

Another potentially serious consequence of GE foods that has not been investigated is the effect of feeding more than one variety of GE plant. If your diet contains GE corn and soy you could be getting two or more different GE genes. Even a single plant, like corn, can contain more than one foreign gene. The effects of these multiple foreign genes can have a significant effect. In medicine this is referred to polypharmacy—the simultaneous use of two or more drugs.

For example, if you feed somebody an aspirin, the side effects might be so minor it is of little concern. However, if you feed that person another drug at the same time, the two drugs can interact to have very serious consequences. The same can be true with GE foods. We don't know because there have not been any such studies.

Very few real safety studies have been done, primarily because of the difficulty of obtaining GE seeds to study. It is nearly impossible for an independent researcher to get GE seeds to verify the results or to make any meaningful investigation.

Independent researchers who wish to do GE studies are forbidden to use GE crops. It is almost impossible for an independent researcher to obtain GE seeds to do safety studies not authorized or funded (i.e., controlled) by the biotech companies. GE seeds are protected by patent laws. You can't simply go down to your local garden store and purchase the seeds. You must get them directly from the biotech companies. Farmers or anyone else who buys the seeds are required to sign a technology user agreement, which obligates the buyer not do any research on the seeds or give the seeds to anyone else to do research. Such precautions make you wonder why the biotech companies are so afraid of having independent research on their products, are they trying to hide something?

## HEALTH DANGERS OF GE FOODS

Genetic engineering is not as precise or as accurate as it is generally believed. The genes from foreign organisms are not carefully inserted into the host's DNA at precise locations for optimal function. When scientists inject the gene into the host, they have no control over where the gene may end up on the host's DNA. This is a potentially serious situation as the position the genes occur on the DNA strand can be important. In other words, genetic engineering is like playing Russian Roulette. You don't know what your results will be. The seeds developed from GE may live, and develop much like an ordinary plant, but the chemical changes within the plant are really unknown and could have far reaching effects on our health, especially if they are eaten over a lifetime.

These chemical changes can alter the nutritional content, effect enzyme structure and activity, and produce various compounds that could be toxic. Many plants produce natural toxins to discourage predators (bugs and animals) from eating them. Ordinarily, we can tolerate a small amount of these toxins, an unnatural gene can possibly alter them causing them to be more toxic or more abundant in the plant and thus, harmful for humans and animals. The foreign gene could cause totally new chemicals to be created that could have drastic effects on our health and the health of the environment. Genetic engineering of our foods is really a massive experiment on the human population. We don't know all the dangers. However, some alarming facts have been uncovered.

Despite the difficulties of independent researchers studying GE foods, a very small handful of studies have been done, with alarming results.

One of the first indications that GE foods might be harmful came from the observations of Howard Vlieger, a crop and livestock nutrition advisor.[4] His first experience with genetically modified organisms (GMOs) came in 1997 when he planted a test plot comparing GE corn to the conventional version. He had heard from farmers in Nebraska that cows shied away from the GE corn. So he gave his cows the choice to consume the conventionally grown corn or GE corn. His cows ate the conventionally grown, however they smelled the GE corn and walked away from it. It's not normal for hungry cattle to refuse food. He has tried this with many other animals and found that if they have not been forced to consume GE food in the past, they won't eat it and will go for the conventional feed instead.

In his role as a crop and livestock nutrition adviser, Vlieger knew other farmers who were feeding their animals

GE feed. In South Dakota, a farmer fed his sows GE corn and they had on average 1.6 less piglets per litter. The piglets also weighed less at birth.

A farmer from Harlan, Iowa, had sows with pseudo pregnancies. They seemed to be pregnant, but when they delivered, there was only a sack of water, afterbirth, and no pigs. The Farm Bureau Spokesman wrote about this farmer's travails and he got calls from other farmers saying they were having the same problem. Interestingly, they were all using the same GE corn. Iowa State University claimed not to find any connection between the GE corn and fertility, but when the farmers stopped using that form of GE corn and switched to conventional corn, the problem disappeared.

Vlieger worked with a hog operation in Nebraska which used GE corn in the feed of breeding animals and found conception rates drop 30 percent. The local vet came out and tested the feed for mycotoxins and mold, but did not find any. The next group of sows was fed conventional corn and conception rates jumped back up to about 90 percent. They switched back to GE corn and conception rates dropped again, this time down by 70 percent.

In Iowa, farmers found anemia and gastrointestinal tract problems such as ileitis (inflammation of the small intestine), bloody bowel, ulcers, and salmonella. When GE corn was taken out of the feed, the problems went away.

If GMOs are causing stomach and gastrointestinal inflammation, bloody bowel, ileitis, infertility, ulcers, and false pregnancies in farm animals, *what are they doing to us?* *If* glyphosate, which is on all GE crops, kills the bacteria in the soil, what does it do to the environment inside our gastrointestinal tract?

Vlieger's observations sparked Judy Carman, PhD to do an in-depth study with pigs to see if the farmer's experiences were truly related to consuming GE crops. Dr. Carman is an adjunct associate professor at Flinders University in South

Australia and the director of the Institute of Health and Environmental Research.[5]

Pigs have a very similar digestive system to humans and what is seen in them when they eat GE foods will likely be found in humans. She wanted to do a proper study with enough pigs to have a statistical significance and for a long enough time to be meaningful. Her first obstacle to overcome was legally obtaining GE seeds. The biotech companies would not sell them to her for her study so she had to devise a means to get them another way. After a great deal of effort, she was able to acquire seeds legally for her study. She declines to reveal how she obtained the seeds because she does not what that loophole to be plugged.

She and her colleagues obtained piglets as soon as they were weaned. The first solid food they were given was either GE or non-GE. The pigs were fed for the entire commercial lifespan. This was a commercial piggery study, it was done under commercial piggery conditions. The animals, once they reached 5 months were processed according to industry standards. So the pigs were exposed to the GE feed for less than 5 months.

Unlike industry sponsored studies that use only a handful of rats, she used a total of 168 pigs in her study, enough to derive some statistical significance in the results.

Carman's study found many of the same problems reported by Vlieger. There was a significant increase in stomach inflammation in the pigs—severe inflammation. "When I say 'severe,' I'm talking about a stomach that is swollen and cherry red in color over almost the entire surface of the stomach," says Carman. "This is not the sort of stomach that you or I would want to have at all."

They next looked a reproductive health. They couldn't examine male reproductive health because all the boars were neutered at 3 days of age. But they could examine the female pigs. They found an abnormal thickening of the uterus in the pigs feed GE food. The uterus was 25 percent heavier. In the paper they talk about all of the disease states that this could represent.[6]

Your body houses some 100 trillion bacteria. You have more bacteria in your body than you have cells, 10 times more. In essence, we are a colony of microbes. These organisms are not simply freeloaders feeding off our bodies, but work in harmony with our bodies performing a wide variety of important functions essential for good health. The type of bacteria in your gastrointestinal (GI) tract is just as important as your own cells for proper digestive function. Some bacteria produce essential vitamins for us, other help us digest foods or strengthen our immune system. Some microbes, including viruses and yeasts, can be harmful and wreak havoc on our bodies if their numbers get out of hand. Having large populations of so-called "friendly" bacteria prevent the overgrowth of potentially harmful microbes. Without these tiny organisms we could not exist, with the wrong type we become prone to malnutrition and disease. Having the right proportions of the different bacteria and other microbes helps keep us healthy.

One of the very serious dangers of GE crops is the alteration of the gut microbiota—the microorganisms living in your GI tract. The studies by Howard Vlieger and Judy Carman demonstrated that diets containing GM foods lead to severe GI inflammation and damage. While it is possible that something in the GM foods could be irritating the GI tract causing these conditions, another possibility is that the high percentage of glyphosate residue on these foods is causing it. We know glyphosate kills soil bacteria, why not gut bacteria as well? These GE chemicals and herbicides could be killing the beneficial gut bacteria, allowing more virulent strains to proliferate, creating an environment in the gut leading to inflammation, leaky gut, ulcers, bleeding, immune disorders, allergies, nutrient malabsorption, and reduced nutrient syntheses, among other things.

Another rare study by an independent researcher was conducted by Dr. Gilles-Eric Seralini. He replicated the studies that the industry used to establish the safety of the GE foods. But rather than terminating the study at three months or less, he took it to two years, which is the typical life expectancy of a rat. In order to obtain statistical significance, Seralini's study included 200 rats, unlike the typical 10 or 20 used in biotech supported studies.

There were some very significant differences between Seralini's study and the previous industry-sponsored studies. Rats fed GE food their entire lives developed huge breast tumors and suffered from liver and kidney damage. As much as 80 percent of the female rats developed large tumors by the beginning of the 24th month, with up to three tumors per animal. Up to 70 percent of female rats died prematurely. Large tumors began to appear after only seven months.

However, the majority of tumors were detectable only after 18 months, meaning they could be discovered only in long-term feeding trials.

Since GE foods are always contaminated with residual glyphosate the effect may possibly have been due to the herbicide rather than the genetic alternation. To identify this possibility Seralini separated the rats into groups. He had some rats fed the GE and non-GE foods without glyphosate contamination, and others were fed foods sprayed with glyphosate. He found that there were problems with animals fed the glyphosate and those fed the non-sprayed GE food, but when you put the two of them together, the effects were worse.[7]

Digestive disorders are becoming rampant—sensitivity to wheat and gluten, celiac disease, food allergies, Crohn's, colitis, and GERD. Such conditions appear to be epidemic. Food allergies are becoming more common. Reproductive health is becoming a growing concern. Infertility, miscarriages, premature births, cesarean deliveries, birth defects, and childhood developmental disorders are at an all time high.

Cancer is the second leading cause of death. We've been at war with cancer for over 40 years and are losing the battle. Are GE crops and pesticides to blame? Until the biotech companies allow independent researchers to do meaningful safety studies we won't know for sure, but the evidence so far suggest it may be so.

## COCONUT OIL TO THE RESCUE

The most common GE crops in the US, Canada, and elsewhere are soybeans, corn, canola, and cottonseed—all of which are used to make edible oils. The cooking oils, shortenings, and margarines you purchase at the grocery store, the oils used in most all of the packaged, canned, and frozen foods you buy, and the oils used in the vast majority of restaurants come from GE crops. The oils in our diet are the most prevalent source of GE foods in our diet.

In the US and many other countries there currently are no laws that require food manufacturers to identify on the labels of their products that they contain GE ingredients. How do you avoid these oils? One way is to purchase "certified organic" products. Organically raised crops, by definition, are those that have been raised and processed without exposure to pesticides and other chemicals. Since GE crops are designed specifically to withstand heavy doses of pesticides, they are naturally heavily sprayed. Therefore, no GE ingredients should be in a certified organic product. Be aware that the word "Natural" on a label does not mean organic. This term has no official meaning, so any product can use the word "Natural" regardless of where the ingredients come from or how they are produced.

If you are mindful of the types of fats and oils you use, you can avoid all of the oils that are tainted with GE ingredients and pesticides. Coconut oil provides a safe and healthful alternative to all these other products. Coconut oil is chemically very stable, has a long shelf life, and is stable under ordinary cooking temperatures making it a suitable replacement for all cooking, baking, and frying uses. No genetically altered coconuts are used for commercial purposes. Nor are they treated with chemical fertilizers or pesticides. Most all coconut products—oil, meat, milk, and such—are produced from organically grown coconuts, even if the products are not officially "certified' organic. Coconut farmers rarely use pesticides. Using coconut oil in place of soybean, corn, canola, cottonseed, and other vegetable oils is good for the environment and good for your health.

## MOST VEGETABLE OILS ARE DESTROYING THE PLANET

Worldwide more land is being destroyed for soybean, canola, and corn oil production than any other crop. Soybean cultivation is the biggest offender and is decimating the Amazon rainforest. Between 3,000 to 5,000 square miles (7,900 to 12,900 sq km) of rainforest is leveled in the Amazon each year, most of it for soybean cultivation.

Brazil holds about 30 percent of the Earth's remaining tropical rainforest. The Amazon Basin produces roughly 20 percent of the Earth's oxygen, creates much of its own rainfall, and harbors many unknown species. The Brazilian rainforest is the world's most biologically diverse habitat. Close to 20 percent of the Amazon rainforest has already been cut down.

Industrial-scale soybean producers are joining loggers and cattle ranchers, speeding up destruction and further fragmenting the great Brazilian wilderness. Between the years 2000 and 2005, Brazil lost more than 50,000 square miles (125,000 sq km) of rainforest. That is equivalent to an area the size of the state of New York. A large portion of that was for soybean farming.

Soybean production in the Brazilian Amazon soared after heat-tolerant varieties were introduced in 1997. In just ten years, exports of soybeans grown in the Amazon Basin reached 42 million tons a year. Total annual soybean production in Brazil is about 85 million tons. Brazil will soon surpass the United States as the world's leader in soybean production.

At the current rate of clearing, scientists predict that 40 percent of the Amazon will be destroyed and a further 20 percent degraded within two decades. If that happens, the forest's ecology will begin to unravel. Intact, the Amazon produces half its own rainfall through the moisture it releases into the atmosphere. Eliminate enough of that rain through clearing, and the remaining trees dry out and die. Currently trees are being wantonly burned to create open land for soybean cultivation. Consequently, Brazil has become one of the world's largest emitters of greenhouse gases.

There are few paved roads into the Amazon. The most controversial is the 1,100 mile long BR-163 highway which runs straight into the heart of the Amazon Basin providing an alleyway for industrial-sized soybean operations to grab up millions of acres of land. Because of the thousands of tons of soy transported over this road it is nicknamed the "soy highway."

The decimation of the Amazon is, for the most part, done legally. Even the governor of the state of Mato Gross, on the southern edge of the Amazon Basin is a part of it. Governor Blairo Maggi is the world's largest single soybean producer, growing 350,000 acres. That's equivalent to 547 square miles (1,370 sq km) of Amazon rainforest that has been leveled for soybean production. He is just one of many industrial-sized soybean operations in the area.

Clearing the land for soybean production is only part of the problem. Soybean cultivation destroys habitat for wildlife including endangered or unknown species. It

*Thousands of acres in the Amazon rainforest are being cleared every year for GE soybean production.*

increases greenhouse gases, which are believed to contribute to global warming and disrupts the life of indigenous tribes who depend on the forest for food and shelter. Soybeans need large amounts of acid-neutralizing lime, as well as fertilizers, pesticides, and herbicides. All of which are creating an environmental hazard. Toxic chemicals contaminate the forest, poison rivers, and destroy wildlife. Indigenous communities complain about poisoned water and dying fish.

The environmental destruction caused by soybean farming isn't limited to the Amazon, it occurs throughout the world wherever soybeans are produced. That's hundreds of thousands of acres of deforestation, over cultivation and destruction of the land, and billions of tons of toxic chemicals spewed into the environment year after year, contaminating our soils, water, and destroying wildlife, not to mention what it is doing to us. New genetically modified soy was specifically developed to withstand the toxins so farmers could spray even more pesticides on them without diminishing yields.

Talk about destroying the environment, the soybean industry has to rank near the top of the offender's list.

## COCONUTS ARE ENVIRONMENTALLY FRIENDLY

Now, let's take a look at how coconut cultivation affects the environment. When you compare soy cultivation to that of coconut, there is a huge difference. Coconut cultivation is one of the world's most environmentally friendly commercial crops. After coconut palms reach maturity—between 5 to 10 years—they are commercially productive for over half a century and continue to produce fruit for about 80 years. That means that once the trees are planted, the soil remains essentially undisturbed for decades. Unlike soy and other crops, were the ground is dug up and recultivated every year, year after year. The soil in a coconut plantation remains essentially undisturbed. Native grasses and foliage are allowed to repopulate the space between trees. Much of the natural habitat remains as it was. A coconut plantation becomes a forest, filled with vegetation and wildlife. Since the ground is continually covered with trees and growth, the soil is not eroded, maintaining the integrity of the environment from the tiniest soil organisms to the largest land animals. So a coconut plantation blends into the environment without causing untold disruption.

Coconut is one of the world's most efficient oil-producing crops in terms of land utilization, efficiency, and productivity. Unlike most other crops that produce once a year, coconut palms produce fruit year round, so coconuts are always in season. This allows for a high yield of fruit on comparatively little acreage. For this reason, the coconut palm produces more oil per acre than just about any other vegetable source. For example, in 1 year on one acre of land a farmer can produce 18 gallons of corn oil, or 35 gallons of cottonseed oil, or 48 gallons of soybean oil. However, on the

*Coconut palms produce fruit year round and are productive for about 80 years.*

same amount of land he can produce 287 gallons of coconut oil! In terms of land use, you would need to plant 6 acres of soy or 16 acres of corn to produce an equal amount of oil from just 1 acre used to grow coconut.

Soybean cultivation requires 6 times more land to produce the same amount of oil. Corn requires 16 times as much land. And this land is stripped of all other vegetation, and continually plowed and replowed, and poisoned with pesticides. On the other hand, coconut palms are planted once and then the land is allowed to return mostly to its natural state without harming the environment. The trees can be productive for nearly a century without any further disturbance to the ground. Many coconut palms used for commercial purposes are harvested in the wild so there is no disturbance to the soil at all. The vast majority of soy, corn, and other oil crops are genetically modified so that they can withstand enormous amounts of pesticides that poison the environment. Genetically modified crops themselves are

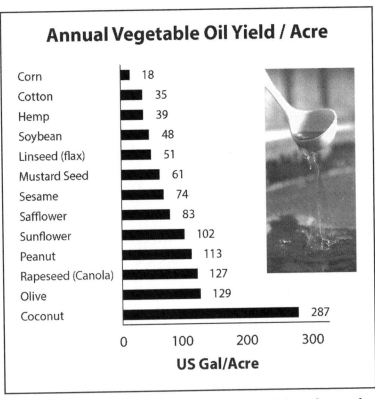

## Annual Vegetable Oil Yield / Acre

| Crop | US Gal/Acre |
|------|------------|
| Corn | 18 |
| Cotton | 35 |
| Hemp | 39 |
| Soybean | 48 |
| Linseed (flax) | 51 |
| Mustard Seed | 61 |
| Sesame | 74 |
| Safflower | 83 |
| Sunflower | 102 |
| Peanut | 113 |
| Rapeseed (Canola) | 127 |
| Olive | 129 |
| Coconut | 287 |

*Coconut palms yield up to 16 times more oil than these other plant sources.*

adversely affecting the environment and the health of animals and people that eat these corps. In contrast, the coconut palm is not genetically modified so it is not sprayed with tons of pesticides, and generally is not sprayed at all.

The coconut palm is a hearty plant and can grow in areas where other food crops cannot. The two things coconut palms need most to survive is a warm climate and adequate moisture. Although they grow best in loamy soil rich in organic matter, they can grow well in poor rocky, sandy, and salty soils. Many small volcanic islands have only a few inches of topsoil and cannot support the growth of most other fruit-bearing plants, but they are covered in coconut palms. The palms can easily take root in the sandy, salty beach soil and thrive. For this reason, coconut palms can be grown and even be commercially productive in many areas that are unproductive and economically infeasible for other food crops.

Coconut palms are plentiful throughout the tropics, so much so they grow like weeds. When planted in large numbers

*Coconuts can germinate and thrive in poor soils.*

*A view looking down on a coconut plantation in Thailand. You can't tell the difference between the plantation and the surrounding rainforest.*

they form palm forests that blend into the tropical landscape. In fact, many tropical rainforests are naturally populated with coconut palms. It is tragic that the Amazon rainforest is being destroyed to cultivate soy, when coconut palms could produce the same amount of oil on just a fraction of the land—land that has already been used for cultivation for many decades, allowing the vast majority of the land to revert back to its native rainforest and the rest of the Amazon to remain unadulterated. Like the native trees in the Amazon, coconut palms would support the natural Amazonian environment, its wildlife, and its unique relationship with the climate in the area. Yet, could supply food and medicine for the locals and produce enough oil to provide them with a decent living—all without harming the environment.

# 4

# A Clean All-Purpose Industrial Oil

## COCONUT OIL FOR CLEAN AIR

Coconut oil has gained recognition as a safe and natural product with a multitude of uses. It has proven valuable in treating a variety of health concerns ranging from psoriasis to obesity. Coconut oil is used in food preparation and as a skin lotion, sun block, healing salve, lip moisturizer, hair conditioner, and dietary supplement. It's also a primary ingredient in many soaps, lotions, and beauty products.

Another remarkable benefit is that it can help protect the lungs from the dangers of air pollution. How can it accomplish this incredible feat? It can do this as a fuel additive or fuel replacement to power automobiles and generators. Coconut oil is an amazingly clean source of energy that can significantly reduce air pollution.

The technical feasibility of using coconut oil in diesel engines has been successfully demonstrated in trials in many Asian and Pacific countries. The use of coconut oil in diesel engines is not new. Vegetable oils have been used to power diesels for years. In fact, the inventor of the diesel engine, Rudolf Diesel, ran his original engine in the 1890s on peanut oil.

Coconut oil has been used periodically throughout the South Pacific for decades. It was used extensively in the Philippines during the Second World War when diesel was in short supply. Since then, the wide availability of diesel throughout the world and difficulties in running engines on coconut oil in cooler weather virtually ended its use in this way. In recent years, however, there has been a revival of interest. This is due to the growing demand for fuel, frequent shortages, and increasing energy prices. There are also concerns about environmental pollution caused by the use of petroleum-based fuels.

Probably no one is more experienced in using coconut oil to power automobiles than 52-year-old Australian born mechanic Tony Deamer. Now living in Vanuatu—a small island nation in the South Pacific—Deamer has championed the use of coconut oil as an alternative source of fuel for many years.

Coconut oil has many advantages over petroleum, including a smoother ride with plenty of power. "Rounding a corner and heading up a steep hill outside the capital of Port Vila," writes one reporter, "Tony Deamer stomped on the gas pedal of his Range Rover—but didn't downshift. With nary a sputter or a cough, the vehicle—modified to run on coconut oil instead of diesel fuel—took the incline in stride."[1]

"Coconut oil is a bit more torquey, because it burns slower," says Deamer, "Normally, I'd have to shift down into first gear, but with coconut oil, I can keep it in second."

Among the other advantages: it doesn't make black smoke, it is less costly (at least in the South Pacific), it has the potential to stimulate employment among local coconut growers, and, perhaps most importantly for the world at large, it is an environmentally friendly fuel. And, according to Deamer, cars burning it can be fun to drive.

Deamer has succeeded in proving that automotive diesel engines, with very little modification, can run safely on pure coconut oil as well as coconut oil/petroleum mixes.

Some 200 minibuses in Vanuatu are using a coconut oil/ diesel mix on a daily basis. Deamer runs his fleet of rental vehicles on a blend of 85% coconut oil and 15% kerosene. Countries such as Thailand and the Philippines are using coconut oil based fuels in many of their government owned vehicles.

The main drawback with using coconut oil is that it solidifies at temperatures below 76° F (24° C). When it becomes solid it can't flow through the fuel lines and filters. This is a definite problem in temperate climates and even in many places in the tropics where temperatures can drop below this point at night.

Outside the tropics, where temperatures dip below 76° F, as much as 20 percent coconut oil can be mixed with diesel without any modifications to the engine. However, if you use pure coconut oil or a coconut oil/diesel mix over 20 percent, there needs to be some modification to the fuel system. This problem is overcome by using either a twin tank system or a pre-heater fitted to the fuel line. In the twin tank system one tank is used for diesel and another for coconut oil. The engine is started and stopped on diesel. The exhaust or coolant hoses are run through the coconut oil tank to heat it. When the oil reaches a safe operating temperature an automatic switchover device changes the supply from diesel to coconut oil. An advantage of this system is no coconut oil is left in the engine which might solidify in the injectors when the engine is stopped and cooled down. With a pre-heater on the fuel line, pure coconut oil or a coconut oil/diesel mix can be fed from a single tank.

There are numerous benefits to using coconut oil. If the oil is produced locally it can be cheaper than imported fuel. This can have a significant economic impact by lowering energy costs and providing employment to locals to harvest coconuts and produce the oil. Unlike fossil fuels which are being depleted, coconut oil is a renewable energy source that is virtually unlimited. Coconut oil is easy to use. It works in diesel engines without any major modifications. Coconut oil enhances fuel economy, performance, and endurance and is environmentally friendly.

Different vegetable oils are being tested around the world as alternative sources of fuel. Most vegetable oils, however, must be converted to biodiesel to be of any practical use. Unaltered polyunsaturated vegetable oils like soybean and linseed oils undergo chemical changes in the engine forming tough epoxy-like deposits that can clog valves, injectors, and pistons and cause loss of power and excessive wear.

Coconut oil is chemically more stable than other oils and has better burning properties making it, without question, the best oil for diesel use. Unlike most other vegetable oils, diesel engines can run on 100 percent coconut oil or a mixture of coconut oil and diesel or coconut biodiesel. Biodiesel is produced through a process called transesterification in which coconut oil is made to react with alcohol, forming an ester— coconut methyl ester or coconut biodiesel. Coconut biodiesel

*Coconut biodiesel is being used in public and government vehicles in many countries. This is one of the trucks operated by the Philippine Department of Agriculture.*

can be substituted completely for diesel or blended with it. Because production is relatively expensive, it is generally mixed with diesel.

Coconut oil burns more slowly than diesel, which results in a more even pressure applied to the pistons during their movement in the cylinders of the engine. This in turn leads to less engine wear, a quieter engine and better fuel economy. Also, as the coconut oil burns slower and has better lubricating qualities than diesel, the engine does not get as hot and there is less wear, which helps to prolong engine life. Under-revving of the engine is also less of a problem, so it is not always necessary to shift down the gears when slowing down or climbing hills, which makes for easier driving and less wear on the gearbox. Trials lasting over one year, using unprocessed coconut oil and diesel mixtures, have confirmed decreased wear on the engine and components compared with using diesel on its own.

Coconut oil acts as a lubricant and solvent. It increases lubricity of the fuel by 36 percent thus reducing wear and tear on the engine. It increases solvency of the fuel which dissolves carbon deposits in the combustion chamber and declogs fuel nozzles, lines, and ports allowing for greater engine efficiency. It also enhances cold starting efficiency of diesel fuel.

Coconut oil is an excellent additive for reducing air pollution. Even a small amount can make a very significant difference. Diesel fuel blended with just 1 percent coconut oil reduces emissions considerably. Studies conducted in Japan and Korea show that emission of particulate matter is reduced by as much as 60 percent and nitrogen oxide (a major pollutant) by 20 percent and smoke is reduced by 70 percent. Adding 2 percent coconut oil lowers pollution even more with smoke emission decreasing by an incredible 90 percent![2-3] A 20 or 50 percent mixture improves these values even more making coconut oil a ideal green fuel.

Coconut oil burns clean producing only carbon dioxide and energy. "One of the reasons I like using coconut oil instead of diesel fuel," says Deamer "is you are putting back into the atmosphere the same carbon dioxide that the tree took out a year ago." Burning coconut oil does not increase atmospheric carbon dioxide because it is essentially recycled back into the trees. "It's completely sustainable," says Deamer. "Coconut trees are very efficient carbon absorbers." And unlike petroleum, coconut oil is completely non-toxic. "What other Pacific fuel can you cook your fish and chips in and run your truck on?"

## COCONUT OIL POWERS BOEING 747

Coconut oil has proven to be a highly efficient and environmentally clean source of energy. Because of these advantages coconut oil is being tested as a jet fuel.

Virgin Atlantic airlines carried out the world's first flight of a commercial aircraft powered with a biofuel made from coconut oil in 2008. The Boeing 747 flew from London to Amsterdam. Neither the jet nor the engines needed to be redesigned or altered for this test flight.

"This breakthrough will help Virgin Atlantic to fly its planes using clean fuel sooner than expected," Sir Richard Branson, the airline's president, said before the Boeing 747 flew from London's Heathrow Airport to Amsterdam's Schiphol Airport. He said the flight provides "crucial knowledge that we can use to dramatically reduce our carbon footprint."

The flight was partially fueled with a biofuel mixture of coconut and babassu oil in one of its four main fuel tanks. The jet carried pilots and several technicians, but no passengers. The flight is an example of how the world's airlines are trying to find ways of reducing aviation's carbon footprint. These efforts have included finding alternative jet fuels, developing

*Coconut oil powers a Boeing 747 in flight from London to Amsterdam.*

engines that burn existing fuels more slowly, and changing the way planes land.

Aircraft engines cause noise pollution and emit gases and particulates that reduce air quality and contribute to environmental pollution. Using coconut oil as a jet and diesel fuel can help keep our planet clean.


**COCONUT MOTOR OIL**

Coconut oil is not only good for powering engines, but for lubricating them as well. Motor vehicle owners in India are already doing it.

In India the streets are littered with small three-wheeled taxis known as autorikshaws. One autorikshaw driver in the town of Cherupuzha has been using coconut oil in his vehicle for years. The driver, G. Rajeevan, says it makes an ideal substitute to more conventional motor oil. Rajeevan's claims have been evaluated by the State Science & Technology Department, which has affirmed that coconut oil could be used as an effective alternative motor oil for small automobile engines stating, "There are no adverse effects on the engine parts or in the performance of the petrol engine." They have, therefore, recommended that coconut oil "can be used as an alternative to the commercial petroleum lubricant" in light commercial vehicles.

This endorsement came after Mr. Rajeevan sent a report about his innovation to Chief Minister Oommen Chandy who Rajevan said, followed up with the State Council for Science, Technology, and Environment. The new lubricant is more environmentally friendly and less expensive than petroleum-based lubricants.

Mr. Rajeevan has been using coconut oil in his autorikshaw for the past 13 years, providing a long term test of the oil in a heavily used commercial vehicle. Autorikshaw drivers depend on their vehicles for their livelihoods. So it is imperative that their vehicles provide trouble-free performance for as long as possible. Coconut oil apparently has passed the test.

Mr. Rajeevan can now seek support of the automobile manufacturing units to profess his claims supported by the State Science & Technology Department. And the Department

*Autorickshaw used for public transportation in India.*

84

will be happy to come in support of his initiative to help provide an environmentally friendly source of motor oil and support local coconut farmers.


## GENERATES CLEAN ELECTRICITY

In addition to fueling diesel and jet engines, coconut oil can be used to produce electricity. Diesel-powered electric generators can burn pure coconut oil or coconut oil/kerosine mixtures to produce the energy needed to light up a house, and run a refrigerator, air conditioner, a computer, and any other electric household appliance.

Because the exhaust produced from burning coconut oil is far cleaner than diesel or gasoline, electricity is produced cleanly. Pure coconut oil can be used in warm tropical climates, but a mix of coconut oil and kerosine or diesel is needed in more temperate climates.


## EDIBLE FUEL AND OIL

When you were growing up did your mother ever tell you to "Eat your vegetables"? Today she may add "and your diesel fuel," if the fuel she's talking about is coconut oil. Could you have ever imagined edible diesel fuel and motor oil? What a novel concept. Wouldn't it be great if all petroleum products were replaced with coconut oil-based products that were safe enough to eat?

You've heard the saying "don't put anything on your skin that is not safe enough to eat." That makes sense because the skin is a living breathing organ that absorbs many of the substances put on it.

Have you ever filled your gas tank or changed your engine oil and come away with your hands or clothes smelling like gas and oil? Some of it invariable spills and gets on our skin and clothes—not good for our skin or our clothes. Petroleum-based gasoline and motor oil are toxic. We don't need them being absorbed into our skin or spilled all over the environment.

However, coconut oil can function very well as a replacement for diesel fuel and motor oil. Use the oil to fry your eggs and hash browns in the morning then pour the rest into your gas tank or engine block. If you spill some in the process, no worries, the oil will degrade like any natural food does and won't contaminate the environment. The fuel will burn clean without the disgusting carbon monoxide smell but produce an aroma more akin to French fries or popcorn.

Other potentially toxic petroleum-based products such as household lubricants, makeup remover, petroleum jelly, lamp fuel, lip balm, rust inhibitor, hydraulic press fluid, and solvents can be replaced with coconut oil. Coconut oil makes a very effective solvent or degreaser for grease-caked hands. Rubbing a little coconut oil on the hands dissolves the grease so that most of it wipes off easily and with a little soap (coconut oil based of course) and water completely cleans the hands. If you spill coconut oil on your skin there is no need to wash up, just rub it in. The oil will soften and nourish your skin.

# 5

# Changing People's Lives

**THE KOKONUT PACIFIC STORY**
On many islands throughout the Pacific and elsewhere, there are few resources available by which communities can make money to pay for much needed food, medicine, and education, let alone things such as roads and electricity. Coconuts are the primary resource in these areas, but until recently the only market for coconut was as copra (sun dried coconut) for the production of refined coconut oil. Revenue from copra, however, has been so small that these communities have struggled in virtual poverty for decades.

In an attempt to help relieve worldwide poverty, efforts have been made to establish other types of industries in these communities that would be self-sustaining. In recent years the demand for coconut oil and other coconut products has increased dramatically. This has provided a means by which many small communities throughout the tropical world could make a living. This surge of interest in coconut led Australian Dan Etherington, PhD to develop the Direct Micro Expelling (DME) process of producing virgin coconut oil. This process is relatively inexpensive and allows small communities to produce their own virgin coconut oil for export to bring in revenue, for their own use in cooking and body care, and for fuel to power generators and automobiles. Each community independently owns and operates their own business.

Through the production of virgin coconut oil, many communities around the world have been able to pull themselves out of poverty. Dan and his company, Kokonut Pacific, have provided the equipment and training for many of these small scale virgin coconut oil operations. For his service to international trade, particularly the design, manufacture, and distribution of coconut oil extraction technology, and through contributions to sustainable agricultural and economic development in the South Pacific region, Dan Etherington was awarded the Order of Australia, the country's highest civilian honor. Below is Dan's story told in his own words.

**How We Got Started**

In 1992 a village soap-maker in Mozambique appealed to a visiting consultancy team to come up with a method of producing oil directly from his community's coconuts. None of the team forgot the plea since, if such a technology existed or could be developed, it could radically transform the lives of poverty-stricken coconut farmers around the world.

Later that year, as an Agricultural Economist at the Australian National University in Canberra and the team leader of the mission to Mozambique, I learnt that the people of a remote Tuvalu island in the middle of the south Pacific had long ago discovered how to cold press coconut oil from sun-dried coconut. However, the copra trade and cheap imported vegetable oils had "killed" this local technology.

Recognising its economic potential, I worked in collaboration with Australia's premier research group (the Commonwealth Science and Industrial Research Organisation - CSIRO) and colleagues to modify Tuvalu's fine-weather household technique into an all-weather cottage-industry technology. We call it Direct Micro Expelling® (DME®) because it produces the oil very quickly, is scaled to work at an individual family farm level, and expels pure virgin coconut oil. The quality of the oil is stunning. With the encouragement and backing of some Christian friends, I helped set up the Kokonut Pacific company to further develop the technology and take it back to the islands. My coconut odyssey actually began in 1976 in Sri Lanka, as described on our website. The journey has been difficult at times but breaking the chains which have been created by the purely extractive copra trade has also been exciting and rewarding.

The DME process produces pure virgin coconut oil (VCO) at the farm household level within one hour of opening the coconuts. The process is very much skill-based but these skills are learnt quite quickly in a "learning by doing" situation. Self-installation using the detailed Kokonut Pacific Training Manuals is also very possible, with appropriate skills.

In 1997 the company began to sell DME equipment, training and consultancy services. There are now many DME units in the South Pacific, Asia and Caribbean countries. The DME technology is helping protect fragile tropical environments by enhancing the incomes and living standards of people from their most sustainable local resource. Villagers are now producing this remarkably pure natural oil (FFA < 0.2%) in commercial quantities. Each unit can produce up to 40 litres of VCO/day while its chemical structure and purity ensures a long shelf life.

## Our Mission

The Company's goal is encapsulated in the motto: "Empowering and bringing hope," Kokonut Pacific works to improve the well-being of the rural population of tropical countries through the production of premium grade coconut oil and other coconut products.

*A typical DME shed in operation in the Solomon Islands.*

This objective is achieved by revitalising the smallholder coconut industry through the use of modern technology and by working in partnership with local communities. In most situations, people want to work and they have plenty of coconuts. Now they have a way of turning those coconuts into very pure, natural, virgin oil within one hour of opening a coconut.

Kokonut Pacific is working hard with local companies, non-government organisations (NGOs) and Governments to make sure that the right support systems are in place.

The capacity of remote communities to produce DME extra virgin coconut oil is often far greater than the local market can absorb. For the dream of regular employment to be realised, other markets have to be found. Because most of the oil has to be exported, this requires organisation for quality control, storage, transport, bulking up and finding buyers. In many cases, these buyers are in other countries so the oil has to be carefully packed and shipped overseas.

We are working with our country partners and international accrediting agencies to gain full organic certification status for the oil. This was first achieved in Samoa. Now this status has also been granted to the operations in the Solomon Islands. Organic certification status is a great encouragement to the producers and assures customers of the quality of the oil. In addition, from the start, we have adopted Full and Fair Trade,

Fair Share, and "triple bottom line" principles (demonstrating care for people, the planet, and profitability).

The greatest advantage that virgin coconut oil has in the islands is that it can substitute for so many products that are currently imported. These include:

**1. Biofuel.** The biggest market for VCO in such remote locations is as a natural biofuel. Coconut oil is rare among vegetable oils in that it can be used directly as a diesel fuel substitute. Typically it is blended with at least 20 percent diesel. This is done to make sure that the fuel is always liquid since pure coconut oil goes solid at temperatures below 25°C. In the Solomons, a 50:50 blend of VCO and diesel is being used more and more extensively to power trucks, tractors and electricity generators.

Kerosene hurricane lamps are a standard feature of most village homes. We have introduced very simple 100 percent VCO lamps using recycled glass jars. This technology is spreading very quickly because it provides a major cash saving for rural households and is a most significant use of VCO as a biofuel.

*Kerosene hurricane lamps are a standard feature in most village homes. These lamps can burn using 100 percent VCO using recycled glass jars. This technology is spreading very quick-ly because it provides a major cash saving for rural households.*

**2. Cooking**. Virgin coconut oil is extremely nutritious and stable as a cooking oil. There are particular health benefits in combining VCO with fish that have a high Omega 3 oil content. Bruce Fife has written a number of books explaining the nutritional and health benefits of VCO for Western diets in contradiction to the misinformation propagated by the multinational oil-seed lobby.

**3. Cosmetic.** Raw VCO is a wonderful natural body moisturiser and massage-oil. However, most people prefer some fragrance. In the Islands, using traditional local knowledge, fragrant flowers, leaves, bark or roots are often crushed, dried and then soaked in the oil.

**4. Soap**. Coconut oil soap is very easy to make and lathers well—even in sea water. This downstream processing is becoming an increasingly significant component of the DME processing and brings us right back to the 1992 plea of the village soap-maker in Mozambique.

**5. Medicinal uses:** As Bruce Fife has been stressing in his many books, regularly eating coconut oil (3 tablespoons/day) boosts the immune system. We are trying to make this a feature of local hospitals' preventive health care. Also, since most coconut producing areas in the world are infested with mosquitoes, malaria is a major health hazard. VCO is a very good carrier oil for insect repellents, for example if it is blended with citronella (which comes from lemon grass) or lavender oil.

The residual coconut meal that is leftover after oil extraction is an excellent stock feed for pigs, cattle, horses, and chickens. The unmilled meal can be used in cakes and biscuits as a de-fatted desiccated coconut for human consumption. It can also be milled to get fine edible flour which can be added to various cake and bread mixes. Coconut flour is becoming popular as a flavoursome, gluten-free, high-fibre alternative to wheat flour.

All of this before we get to the multiple uses of the shells and husk, trunk, flowers and fronds! But that is another story.

Our story started out as an effort to assist smallholder farmers in the tropics to gain greater direct benefits from their most sustainable agricultural resource, the coconut palm. The miracle is that while we were developing the oil-extraction process, people like Bruce Fife and Mary Enig were alerting the world to the health benefits of "virgin coconut oil." The production of VCO from the "Tree of Life" has turned out to have much wider benefits than we could have imagined for both producers and consumers. We chose "Niulife" as the brand name for the VCO we sell because it is pronounced "New Life" and "Niu" is the Polynesian word for coconut—a nice play on words. (Check out our website: www.niulife. com).

**Jimmy's Story**

With almost 1,000 islands spread over the Coral Sea, shipping provides the lifeline for people, goods and vital communication in the Solomon Islands. When problems arise, caused by the weather, breakdowns, management difficulties or other issues, the provincial dweller feels it the most.

Recently Jimmy, a key DME Virgin Coconut Oil producer, found that he was down to his last drum of diesel. Unfortunately, it was near Christmas and all ships had been diverted from regular visits to his island to passenger runs— to reunite families for the holiday season.

He had seen a demonstration of a diesel engine running on 100 percent coconut oil. As an experienced mechanic, Jimmy was impressed but had questions concerning the long term sustainability of the alternative fuel. However, now his tractor needed fuel to continue the Virgin Coconut Oil production and transportation operations that take place in his district.

So, choosing some clean coconut oil that he had recently produced, he mixed up a batch with 50 percent diesel and poured it into the tractor. After repeated fills and regular use in all conditions, the tractor is still running "sweet."

*Jimmy's tractor*

Now the truck, pickup, and small generators for the coconut oil plants are all running on 50 percent coconut oil. Jimmy readily admits that he was forced into taking this action by the need to keep his machines running, but now he uses it all the time. "I always have some oil available" he says. "By using it to supplement my diesel supply, it keeps the fuel costs down and makes us less reliant on the irregular shipping. Besides," he adds with a smile, "it makes less smoke and sure makes the machines smell nicer."

**Linter's Story**

Linter had recently returned to the Solomon Islands from New Zealand where her husband had qualified as a mechanical engineer. While waiting for replies to her job applications, she started to make soap using the simple formulae provided in the Kokonut Pacific Training Manual. Following the success of her early experiments, she added some fragrance and food colouring. A New Zealand friend sent her 20 cutlery trays which made perfect soap moulds. The cured soap-bars found a ready local market. Quite quickly Linter withdrew her job applications and concentrated on soap making.

*Linter's bars of soap ready to be cut, packaged, and shipped.*

## A WAY OUT OF POVERTY

With the production and sale of coconut oil many populations around the world are pulling themselves out of poverty. An example of this is in Inhambane Province, Mozambique, Africa. Inhambane is located on the east coast in the southern part of the country.

One of the last things a visitor would expect to find at the end of a little dirt road that twists through Mozambique's mosquito-infested forest is a factory employing 20 people that makes high-quality organic products. But after an hour-long drive inland from the town of Maxixe in Inhambane Province, Coconut Oil Organics' factory emerges from behind a wall of trees.

Coconut Oil Organics is the brainchild of South African farmer Graham Ford and the American non-profit organization TechnoServe. Coconut Oil Organics supplies customers in South Africa and Mozambique organic food and healthcare products, primarily virgin coconut oil and dried desiccated coconut.

TechnoServ's long-term goal is to aid in the establishment of similar factories across the province, using the abundant supply of coconut trees in the area. The potential to create employment for hundreds, if not thousands, of unemployed rural Mozambicans is significant.

In addition to the employees working at the factory, dozens of local farmers harvest coconuts that grow wild in the area and bring them to the factory to sell for processing, providing an income for many more people. One of the keys to this industry is to ensure the factories remain in rural areas rather than near the highway or in the cities. This means that locals, who travel by foot or use animal pulled carts, have far less distance to carry the coconuts to the factory.

"About 50 locals take two large bags of cleaned coconuts each per week to the factory," says Rizwan Khan an agriculture consultant for TechnoServe. "From the sale they make an extra 1,000 meticais ($28) a month for their family, which is significant here. Inhambane is one of the poorest provinces in Mozambique but there is potential to alleviate the poverty. Until now the local people have not really availed of the natural resources around them on a commercial level. At the highway they were only given small sums by men who cashed in by taking the fruit to Maputo (the capital)."

A government survey in 2003 revealed that Inhambane was the poorest of the country's 11 provinces, with nearly 80 percent living below the poverty line. Not long after the factory was established a follow-up survey was take in 2009 that showed that poverty had been reduced to 60 percent and the province had risen in rank surpassing four other provinces.

Widespread drought has contributed to the poverty rate in the area as many crops are severely affected. However, coconuts are resistant to drought. The periodic droughts that hit the area have little effect on the coconut industry.

Every part of the coconut is used. Nothing goes to waste. It is a totally green process. A byproduct of coconut oil production is the coconut pulp leftover after the extraction process. The pulp is a good source of vitamins, minerals, and fiber and contains a residual amount of health-promoting oil. The pulp makes a healthy organic feed for animals and livestock and can be used to make compost for gardens. The shell of the coconut is not wasted either, it is used as a more efficient fuel, in place of wood, to heat the ovens used to dehydrate and process the dried coconut and coconut oil. This prevents the need to cut down and burn trees for this purpose. The ash leftover after burning can be used as a fertilizer to enrich soils. It's a win-win-win situation.


## COCONUT OIL IS SAVING LIVES

This is a wonderful story that describes how coconut oil is bringing better health to people and in some cases literally saving their lives. This story was told to me by Elizabeth. I'll let her tell her story. in her own words.

My name is Elizabeth Wangari Gachiri. I work at an orphanage in Kenya. I have a wonderful story to tell you about coconut oil.

A week ago I attended a weeklong camp meeting with about 150 other people. One of the teachers was a lady named Miriam. I know her because she was a social worker at the orphanage. Miriam is HIV positive and has been very sick for a number of years. She was wasting away and had lost so much weight that she was literally just skin and bones. Her friends and family expected her to die any day. Suddenly, for seemingly no reason, she started to regain weight and get better. Over the following weeks and months her health continued to improve. No one knew why. We were all mystified by her miraculous recovery.

Her health had improved to such an extent that she was able to participate as one of the instructors at the camp meeting. Here she revealed her secret. During the time she was sick, the orphanage received a donation of hundreds of books from Australia. One of the books was *The Coconut Oil*

*Miriam reading to the audience out of The Coconut Oil Miracle.*

*Miracle* by Dr. Bruce Fife. Intrigued by the title, she began reading it. What she learned stunned her. She was particularly fascinated by the section on the antimicrobial properties of coconut oil and its successful use by those with HIV. By this time, her illness had reduced her to a mere 26 kg (57 pounds). Encouraged by the book, Miriam began eating coconut oil and milk daily. As her health improved, her weight returned to its normal 70 kg (154 pounds). When the doctors saw her remarkable improvement they began asking questions.

At the meeting she was bursting with enthusiasm for what coconut had done for her and was anxious to share her newfound knowledge with those in attendance. She taught them how to prepare coconut milk from coconuts brought in from the coast. Her lecture and demonstration captivated the audience since many there had known her when she was deathly ill. Everyone was excited about the coconut oil.

One mother brought her four-year-old son. His hands, face, and head were covered with some kind of infection. His hands were painfully swollen and covered with oozing sores and pealing skin. He looked an awful sight. A coconut porridge was made and applied to the boy's sores. By the end of the week he was recovering remarkably well. I saw him with his parents at church the following week and could not believe my eyes. When I saw him full of energy and fully recovered from head to toe, oh, I could not hold back my tears! The only traces of the infection are a few spots of lighter coloration from the growth of healing skin.

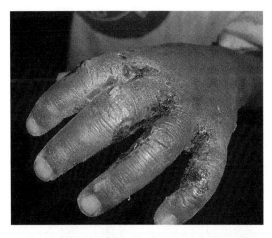

*A four-year-old boy with a spreading skin infection covering his hands, head, and face.*

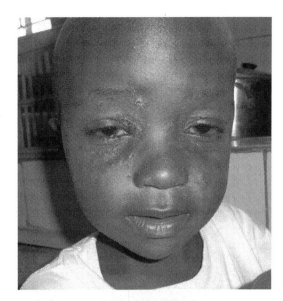

*The skin around the boy's eyes, eyebrows, and cheeks was infected.*

*After rubbing coconut oil on his skin daily for several days the infection completely healed.*

Miriam is very happy to have *The Coconut Oil Miracle* and won't let it out of her hands for a minute. We in Africa are poor and often can't afford medications. This is why so many are dying. We need books like this that offer inexpensive, yet effective alternatives.

## Dr. Fife's Comments

This story is yet another example of the antimicrobial effects of coconut oil and its effectiveness against the HIV virus and other infections. I sent Elizabeth an entire case of *The Coconut Oil Miracle* free of charge to be distributed to those in her community.

After receiving the books she replied: "Thank you for the books and I know God will do miracles with them to help the poor people who are struggling to heal their loved ones but can't afford the medical bills. I will do my best to see that as many people as I can get the message of the coconut oil miracle. For me and my family we are 100 percent and it is working miracles. For the two months that we have used coconut oil on our bodies and eating it daily there has been a

*Elizabeth and her daughter.*

great change as you can see from the picture (on the previous page). My daughter's face is now smooth and pimple free, my husband's face is also smooth. He also used to have dandruff in his hair, he used to scratch his head all the time but now that is no more, thanks to the coconut oil. Because of a sunburn, I had spots on my face. After using coconut oil daily, the spots are fading away. Soon I will have a spotless face thanks to coconut oil."

# 6

# Protecting Marine Life

## SAVING THE SEA TURTLES

The benefits of coconut oil are many. Coconut oil can help improve both physical and mental health, improve the health and appearance of your skin and hair, reduce risk of numerous health problems such as diabetes, cancer, and Alzheimer's, and fight off infections. Another benefit is that it is helping to save endangered sea turtles from extinction.

The leatherback sea turtle is the largest living turtle and the heaviest reptile next to the crocodile. Mature sea turtles are typically between 4 to 6 feet in length and weigh 650 to 1,100 pounds. The turtles have a characteristic leather-like shell and a teardrop-shaped body with a large pair of front flippers to power them through the water.

Adult leatherback sea turtles don't have teeth, but rather delicate, scissor-like jaws. Their jaws would be damaged eating hard foods so they subsist almost entirely on jellyfish; they are one of the few animals that feed on jellyfish. The sea turtles' thick skin, including the skin in their mouth and throat, is impervious to the jellyfish's stings. Consequently, sea turtles are invaluable in controlling jellyfish populations, including the deadly man-of-war.

*Leatherback sea turtle.*

Unfortunately, sea turtles often eat floating plastic bags and other debris which they mistake as jellyfish. The plastic clogs their throats and digestive tract, killing them. Many more are killed when caught in fishing nets.

The turtles leave the water and lay their eggs on land. When the eggs hatch, the baby turtles make a dash to the sea. This is a perilous trip as predators abound and snatch the helpless turtles by the hundreds before they can reach the safety of the ocean. The trip from the nest to the sea is so perilous that only about 1 in 100 survives the journey. Even if they manage to reach the water they remain easy prey to numerous ocean predators for the next several years.

People around the world hunt the sea turtle and harvest its eggs. The love of sea turtle eggs in Asia and Central America has been cited as the most significant factor for the species' global population decline. In Southeast Asia, egg harvesting has lead to a near-total collapse of local nesting populations. For example, in Malaysia, which once had a booming population of sea turtles, they are now nearly extinct. Some biologists have estimated that the leatherback could become extinct within the next 10 years.

*Sea turtle eggs being sold in a Malaysian market.*

Some local communities are now helping to save the leatherback by making coconut oil....Come again? How does making coconut oil help to save sea turtles? It all comes down to economics. Sea turtles and their eggs are harvested and poached by local villagers as a means of making a living. The production and sale of coconut oil creates an alternative source of income for the villagers living along the sea turtles nesting beaches.

The island Barra de Pacuare on the eastern coast of Cost Rica is an example. The island is not a tourist destination and locals have few options for earning income. Poachers have been hunting the eggs for a lifetime and have no other marketable skills. It is difficult to stop them from poaching as they are mostly illiterate and lack any employable skills. However, they are finding the community production of coconut oil to be a workable alternative that provides year round income so that they no longer need to poach sea turtle eggs.

The Casa de Coco (house of coconut) in Costa Rica is a volunteer organization established to teach villagers how to set up, produce, and market coconut oil from the thousands of coconuts that grow wild in the region. Their efforts are turning long time poachers into successful coconut oil producers. Rather than stripping the world of an endangered species, they are now producing a renewable source of food and medicine that benefits everyone, including the sea turtles. Hooray for the coconut!

## SAVING CORAL REEF ECOSYSTEMS

Coral reefs are some of the most diverse ecosystems in the world. Coral polyps, the animals primarily responsible for building reefs, can take many forms: large reef building colonies, graceful flowing fans, and even small, solitary organisms. Thousands of species of corals have been discovered; some live in warm, shallow, tropical seas and others in the cold, dark depths of the ocean.

Because of the diversity of life found in the habitats created by corals, reefs are often called the "rainforests of the sea." About 25 percent of the ocean's fish depend on healthy coral reefs. Fish and other organisms live in the many nooks and crannies formed by corals. The Northwest Hawaiian Island coral reefs, which are part of the Papahānaumokuākea National Marine Monument, provide an example of the diversity of life associated with shallow-water reef ecosystems. This area supports more than 7,000 species of fish, invertebrates, plants, sea turtles, birds, and marine mammals.

Shallow water, reef-building corals have a symbiotic relationship with photosynthetic algae called zooxanthellae, which live in their tissues. The coral provides the zooxanthellae a protected environment and compounds needed for photosynthesis. In return, the algae produce carbohydrates that the coral uses for food, as well as oxygen. The algae also help the coral remove waste.

Coral reefs protect coastlines from storms and erosion, provide jobs for local communities, and offer opportunities for recreation. They are also a source of food and new medicines (see page 108). Over half a billion people depend on reefs for food, income, and protection. Fishing, diving, and snorkeling on and near reefs add hundreds of millions of dollars to local businesses. The net economic value of the world's coral reefs is estimated to be tens of billions of U.S. dollars per year. These ecosystems are culturally important to indigenous people around the world.

*Coral reefs are teaming with life and are often called the rainforests of the sea.*

Unfortunately, coral reef ecosystems are severely threatened. Some threats are natural, such as diseases, predators, and storms. Other threats are caused by people, including pollution, sedimentation, and unsustainable fishing practices. Many of these threats can stress corals, leading to coral bleaching and possible death, while others cause physical damage to these delicate ecosystems.

One source of pollution that is contributing to the destruction of coral reefs come from swimmers. It is not so much the swimmers that are the problem but the sunscreen lotions they use. Sunscreens contain compounds that are toxic to coral reefs. Just a small amount is enough to cause corals to bleach, losing their symbiotic algal energy source and become more susceptible to viral infections.

There are two major categories of sunscreen: physical and chemical. Physical sunscreens contain tiny minerals that act as a shield deflecting the sun's rays. Chemical sunscreens use synthetic compounds that absorb UV light before it reaches the skin. These protectorates wash off in the water. For every 10,000 beach goers, about 4 kilograms of mineral particles

# Medicines From The Sea

If you get a serious bacterial infection, your life may be saved by antibiotics But have you ever wondered where these medicines come from?

Most drugs come from plants on land, but finding new sources is difficult. And some bacteria have become resistant to many of these drugs—so much in fact that these drugs no longer work. The ocean, with its amazing biodiversity, offers more organisms for scientists to develop new medicines.

National Oceanic and Atmospheric Administration (NOAA) scientists and their partners have discovered a chemical that breaks down the shield that some bacteria use to protect themselves from antibiotics. Used as a helper drug, antibiotics that are no longer effective could once again be able to fight off these resistant bacteria.

NOAA scientists have also extracted chemicals from corals and sponges that fight some of the worst infectious bacteria. In order to make these new antibiotics, scientists make copies of these chemicals in a laboratory. This way they don't have to constantly harvest corals from the ocean, leaving our marine ecosystems healthy and intact.

Two marine-derived drugs are already in use—an anti-tumor medication derived from sea squirts and a painkiller from a cone snail. More than a dozen drugs are in clinical trials, including ones to treat Alzheimer's and lung cancer.

The ocean may hold the key for finding new medicines, but not if we don't keep it—and everything that lives there—healthy and pollution free. We need to do our part to protect coral reefs. When swimming, snorkeling, or scuba diving, do not use synthetic sunscreens and do not touch coral beds or the sea floor. The next cure may be hidden there.

Source: https://oceantoday.noaa.gov/medicinesfromthesea/

wash into the ocean. That may not seem like much, but these minerals catalyze the production of hydrogen peroxide, a well-known bleaching agent, at a concentration high enough to harm the reefs.

One of the most common ingredients in chemical sunscreens is oxybenzone, which is toxic to corals, algae, sea urchins, fish, and mammals, including humans. A single drop of this chemical in more than 4 million gallons of water is enough to endanger organisms.

Preservatives used in sunscreens can also be toxic to reefs, as well as humans. Parabens, such as methyl paraben and butyl paraben, are fungicides and antibacterial agents that extend the shelf life of the product. These products also kill the algae that coral reefs depend on.

In 2015, the nonprofit Haereticus Environmental Laboratory surveyed Trunk Bay beach on St. John, US Virgin Islands, where up to 5,000 people swim daily. It was estimated that over 6,000 pounds of sunscreen was deposited on the reef annually. The same year, it found that an average of 412 pounds of sunscreen was deposited daily on the reef at Hanauma Bay, a popular snorkeling destination in Oahu, Hawaii. It is estimated that 14,000 tons of sunscreen is deposited in the ocean annually, with the greatest damage occurring in popular reef areas in Hawaii and the Caribbean.

One solution to this problem is to use the same type of sunscreen lotion the South Pacific islanders have used for generations—coconut oil. Coconut oil, in fact, was the first sunscreen lotion used before the development of synthetic sunscreens. It works very well and is completely nontoxic to the reefs, the wildlife, and you.

## Using Coconut Oil As A Sunscreen

For generations coconut oil was the only sunscreen Pacific islanders used. With a layer of coconut oil on their skin, the scantily clad islanders could spend an entire day under the hot tropical sun without getting sunburned and without ever developing skin cancer.

Coconut oil will protect you too. However, if you eat or have been eating a lot of polyunsaturated vegetable oils your skin will be hypersensitive to the sun and you will burn easily. The oils in our diet get incorporated into our skin. Polyunsaturated oils are unstable and degrade easily when exposed to sunlight, even when they are in our skin, causing the creation of free radicals that promote sunburn and skin cancer.

If your diet contains a lot, or any, polyunsaturated oils, you will be more susceptible to sunburn. Applying coconut oil on the skin will provide some degree of protection, but to gain full protection from the sun, not only do you need to use coconut oil topically, but you need to eliminate *all* polyunsaturated vegetable oils in your diet as well. If your diet includes polyunsaturated vegetable oils, you will only get partial protection from the topical use of coconut oil. You will need to limit your sun exposure and apply coconut oil often. The most common vegetables oils that you should avoid are corn, soybean, safflower, sunflower, cottonseed, and canola oils, and all margarines and shortenings.

If your diet is free from polyunsaturated vegetable oils, and you eat coconut oil as a part of your everyday diet, one or two applications of coconut oil on your skin will protect you from the sun for an entire day.

If you have been eating polyunsaturated vegetable oils, it may take as long as a year or more to completely replace them in your body tissues. So even after you eliminate these oils from your diet and replace them with other healthier oils, such as coconut oil, it may take some time for your body to lose its hypersensitivity to the sun.

# Appendix

# The Coconut Bookshelf

Coconut oil is one of the most environmentally friendly products on the planet with a multitude of uses. It can easily replace many foods, medicines, and industrial products that harm the planet. One of the most remarkable benefits of coconut oil is its use as a food and medicine. If you look at all of the health and nutritional studies that have been done on coconut and coconut oil you will find that coconut oil is not only a health food it is a super health food with health benefits that go far beyond any other food.

The information on coconut oil is huge, so much so that it is impossible to include it all in a single volume. This book provides only a brief overview of some of the major environmental and social benefits of coconut oil. It does not cover all the health conditions that can be benefitted with the use of coconut oil or go into detail as to how to use coconut oil to treat these conditions. Often, simply adding coconut oil into the diet can bring about remarkable changes, but the effects of coconut oil can be greatly enhanced when combined with a proper diet or specific procedures. Topics not covered in this book include how to use the oil topically on the skin and hair, for oral health and how to treat specific health issues. These topics are covered in detail in other books.

In addition to coconut oil, the coconut palm produces several other products, namely coconut meat, milk, water, flour, and sugar. Each of these products provides unique health benefits separate from those of coconut oil. All of them can be used to promote better health. Presented in this appendix is a brief overview of the best books that explain how to use coconut oil and other coconut products to prevent, treat, and reverse many common health issues as well as provide recipes and cooking tips using these products.

**THE COCONUT OIL MIRACLE**
**5th Edition**
*By Bruce Fife, ND*
*Foreword by Jon J. Kabara, PhD*

This was the first book that describes the many health and nutritional benefits of coconut oil. All of the information ipresented in it comes directly from published medical research, the historical record, and the author's own personal experience. This book dispels the untruths surrounding this often misunderstood oil.

Benefits of Coconut Oil include:
• Reduces risk of atherosclerosis and heart disease
• Reduces risk of cancer and other degenerative conditions
• Helps prevent bacterial, viral, and fungal (including yeast) infections
• Supports immune system function
• Helps prevent osteoporosis
• Helps control diabetes
• Promotes weight loss
• Enhances ketogenesis
• Provides an immediate source of energy

- Improves digestion and nutrient absorption
- Has a mild delicate flavor
- Is highly resistant to spoilage (long shelf life)
- Is heat resistant (the healthiest oil for cooking)
- Helps keep skin soft and smooth
- Helps prevent premature aging and wrinkling of the skin
- Helps protect against skin cancer and other blemishes

Coconut oil has been called the healthiest dietary oil on earth. If you're not using coconut oil for your daily cooking and body care needs you're missing out on one of nature's most amazing health products.

"Dr. Bruce Fife should be commended for bringing together in this very readable book the positive health benefits of coconut oil. The inquiring reader will have a new and more balanced view of the role of fat and especially saturated fats in our diet."

Jon Kabara, PhD
Professor Emeritus,
Michigan State University

"He does a fabulous job of documenting how coconut oil, a saturated fat, is actually beneficial to your heart...Fife's book explains in great detail many of the other great healing aspects of this forgotten oil. I heartily recommend you get a copy of the book and study it for yourself."

William Campbell Douglass, MD
*Second Opinion*

**The Coconut Oil Miracle** is available from the publisher at www.piccadillybooks.com or from Amazon at https://goo. gl/GYit3Y.

**COCONUT CURES**
**Preventing and Treating Common Health Problems with Coconut**
*By Bruce Fife, ND*
*Foreword by Conrado S. Dayrit, MD*

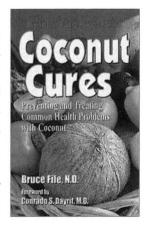

Discover the amazing health benefits of coconut oil, meat, milk, and water. In this book you will learn why coconut oil is considered the healthiest oil on earth and how it can protect you against heart disease, diabetes, and infectious illnesses such as influenza, herpes, Candida, and even HIV. There is more to the healing power of coconut than just the oil. You will also learn about the amazing health benefits of coconut meat, milk, and water. You will learn why coconut water is used as an IV solution and how coconut meat can protect you from colon cancer, regulate blood sugar, and expel intestinal parasites. Contains dozens of fascinating case studies and remarkable success stories. You will read about one woman's incredible battle with breast and brain cancer and how she cured herself with coconut. This book includes an extensive A to Z reference with complete details on how to use coconut to prevent and treat dozens of common health problems.

Statements made in this book are documented with references to hundreds of published medical studies. The foreword is written by Dr. Conrado Dayrit, the first person to publish studies showing the benefit of coconut oil in treating HIV patients.

"As a doctor I have found coconut oil to be very useful. It has been of great help in treating hypertension, high

114

cholesterol, and thyroid dysfunction as well as many other conditions. I highly recommend that you read this book."

Edna Aricaya-Huevos, MD

"Coconut oil has an important medical role to play in nutrition, metabolism, and health care. Indeed, properly formulated and utilized, coconut oil may be the preferred vegetable oil in our diet and the special hospital foods used promoting patient recovery."

Conrado S. Dayrit, MD

"Excellent book. It is very helpful for those seeking to improve their health using natural medicine. I am actively conducting clinical trials and medical research using coconut oil and have seen very positive results with my patients."

Marieta Jader-Onate, MD

*Coconut Cures* is available from the publisher at www. piccadillybooks.com or from Amazon at https://goo.gl/ WfvW4Y.

## OIL PULLING THERAPY
### Detoxifying and Healing the Body Through Oral Cleansing

*By Bruce Fife, ND*

All disease starts in the mouth! As incredible as it may sound, most of the chronic and infectious illnesses that trouble our society today are influenced by the health of our mouths.

Our mouths are a reflection of the health inside our bodies. If you have poor dental health, you are bound to have other health problems. Despite regular brushing and flossing, 98 percent of the population has some degree of gum disease or tooth decay. Most people aren't even aware they have existing dental problems.

Recent research has demonstrated a direct link between oral health and chronic illness. Simply improving the health of your teeth and gums can cure many chronic problems. More brushing, flossing, and mouthwash won't do it. What *will* work is Oil Pulling Therapy. Oil pulling is an age-old method of oral cleansing originating from Ayurvedic medicine. It is one of the most powerful, most effective methods of detoxification and healing in natural medicine.

Dr. Fife's Oil Pulling Therapy is a revolutionary new treatment combining the wisdom of Ayurvedic medicine with modern science. The science behind oil pulling is fully documented with references to medical studies and case histories. Although incredibly powerful, Oil Pulling Therapy is completely safe and simple enough for even a child.

***Oil Pulling Therapy*** is available from the publisher at www.piccadillybooks.com or from Amazon at https://goo.gl/Gehfss.

## THE *NEW* ARTHRITIS CURE
**Eliminate Arthritis and Fibromyalgia Pain Permanently**
*By Bruce Fife, ND*

The title of this book makes a bold statement. It promises a cure. Is this really possible? Yes, there is a cure to arthritis. You can eliminate arthritis and fibromyalgia pain permanently.

This book reveals the true cause of arthritis and fibromyalgia. Up till now these conditions have been considered incurable. The reason for this is that doctors have not recognized the cause, and without knowing the cause it

116

is virtually impossible to develop a cure. Recent medical research, however, has established a clear cause and effect connection. The underlying cause for all the major forms of arthritis and for fibromyalgia is now known.  Drugs aren't the answer. However, there are natural health-promoting therapies that do work and can stop the progression of the disease and encourage regeneration and recovery.

In this book you will read about new groundbreaking medical research, fascinating case studies, and inspiring personal success stories. You will learn about a totally unique approach to overcoming arthritis and fibromyalgia called the Anti-Arthritis Battle Plan. More importantly, you will learn what steps you must take in order to stop the disease process and regain your health.

"Arthritis is not something that must be suffered through. [this book] promotes a new way that could help thousands suffering from the ailment...without the use of drugs."

--*Midwest Book Review*

"An amazing guide... you'll learn the underlying cause of arthritis and...you'll discover the actual cure... I'd recommend *The New Arthritis Cure* to anyone who is interested in a healthier lifestyle and definitely to those who are suffering from arthritis and fibromyalgia."

--Martha Ramirez, *Bookpleasures*

**The New Arthritis Cure** is available from the publisher at www. piccadillybooks.com or from Amazon at https://goo.gl/rK5JuL.

## COCONUT THERAPY FOR PETS

*By Bruce Fife, ND*

What can you do if your cat has worms? Use coconut oil. What can you do about smelly doggy breath? Try coconut oil. What if your cat has an ear infection? Again, coconut oil. Believe it or not, coconut oil is a highly effective treatment for a wide variety of common health problems. For this reason, coconut oil has gained a reputation as a superfood—a food that provides health benefits far beyond it nutritional content.

Coconuts and coconut oil have a long history of safe and effective use as food and as medicine for both humans and animals. Most animals love the taste of coconut. Whether you own cats, dogs, ferrets, parrots, horses, goats, hamsters, gerbils, guinea pigs, rabbits, or other animals, they can all benefit from the nutritional and medicinal properties of coconut oil.

Some of the many health benefits include:

• Reduces or eliminates body odor and bad breath
• Prevents and fights bacterial, viral, and yeast infections
• Improves oral health and whitens teeth
• Helps ease allergy symptoms
• Sooths itchy or irritated skin
• Improves digestion and nutrient absorption
• Protects against digestive disorders such as ulcers and colitis
• Expels or kills intestinal parasites
• Helps prevent and ease joint pain and ligament problems

- Speeds healing from cuts, burns, insect bites, and other injuries
- Protects against fleas, ticks, mites, and other parasites
- Improves the appearance of the skin, hair, and feathers
- Improves energy and balances metabolism
- Helps reduce excess body fat and maintain proper weight
- Strengthens immune function
- Helps relieve kennel cough
- Helps keep blood sugar in balance
- Helps build strong bones

*Coconut Therapy for Pets* is available from the publisher at www.piccadillybooks.com or from Amazon at https://goo.gl/gWJ5J2.

## VIRGIN COCONUT OIL
### Nature's Miracle Medicine
*By Bruce Fife, ND*

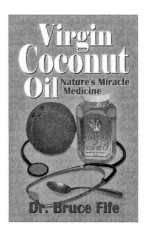

For countless generations virgin coconut oil has been used throughout the world as a nourishing food and a healing medicine. Its therapeutic use is described in ancient medical texts from India, Egypt, and China. Among the Pacific Islanders coconut is regarded as a sacred food. The oil is highly revered for its healing properties and forms the basis for nearly all of their traditional cures and therapies.

Modern medical science is now unlocking the secrets to virgin coconut oil's miraculous healing powers. Coconut oil in one form or another is currently being used in medicines,

119

baby formulas, sports and fitness products, hospital feeding formulas, and even as a weight loss aid. Many doctors and nutritionists consider it to be the healthiest of all oils.

This short 95-page introduction to the miracles of coconut oil is presented in a friendly, non-technical format for those who want the facts but don't want to wade through a lot of scientific explanations and medical facts. Instead, it is filled with fascinating success stories and incredible testimonials from real people in real life situations.

In this book you will discover how people are successfully using virgin coconut oil to prevent and treat high cholesterol, high blood pressure, arthritis, fibromyalgia, Candida, ulcers, herpes, allergies, psoriasis, influenza, diabetes, and much more.

This book makes an excellent companion to *The Coconut Oil Miracle* or *Coconut Cures*. Contains different information.

***Virgin Coconut Oil*** is available from the publisher at www.piccadillybooks.com or from Amazon at https://goo.gl/uK1NTv.


**COCONUT WATER FOR HEALTH AND HEALING**

*By Bruce Fife, ND*

Coconut water is a refreshing beverage that comes from coconuts. It's a powerhouse of nutrition containing a complex blend of vitamins, minerals, amino acids, carbohydrates, antioxidants, enzymes, health enhancing growth hormones, and other phytonutrients.

Because its electrolyte (ionic mineral) content is similar to human plasma, it has gained international acclaim as a natural sports drink for oral rehydration. As such, it has proven superior to commercial sports drinks. Unlike other beverages, it is completely compatible with the human body, in so much that it can be infused directly into the bloodstream. In fact, doctors have used coconut water successfully as an intravenous fluid for over 60 years.

Coconut water's unique nutritional profile gives it the power to balance body chemistry, ward off disease, fight cancer, and retard aging. History and folklore credit coconut water with remarkable healing powers, which medical science is now confirming. Published medical research and clinical observation have shown that coconut water:

- Makes an excellent oral rehydration sports beverage
- Aids in exercise performance
- Aids in kidney function and dissolves kidney stones
- Protects against cancer
- Provides a source of ionic trace minerals
- Improves digestion
- Contains nutrients that feed friendly gut bacteria
- Helps relieve constipation
- Reduces risk of heart disease
- Improves blood circulation
- Lowers high blood pressure
- Improves blood cholesterol levels
- Helps prevent atherosclerosis
- Prevents abnormal blood clotting
- Possesses anti-aging properties
- Restores strength and elasticity to skin
- Reduces discolored aging spots on skin
- Reduces wrinkles and sagging skin
- Enhances healing of wounds and lesions
- Supports good vision and prevents glaucoma

*Coconut Water for Health and Healing* is available from the publisher at www.piccadillybooks.com or from Amazon at https://goo.gl/nq7JA2.

## THE COCONUT MIRACLE COOKBOOK

*By Bruce Fife, N.D.*

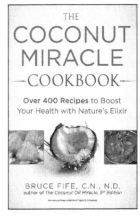

If you like coconut, you will love this book. It's written for coconut lovers as well as for the growing number of health conscious individuals who recognize coconut as a marvelous health food.

Every recipe contains coconut in one form or another. Some recipes such as Coconut Battered Shrimp and Coconut Macaroons use shredded or flaked coconut. Others such as Chicken A La King and Strawberry Chiffon Pie use coconut milk or cream in place of dairy. The salad dressings and mayonnaise recipes are based on coconut milk and oil.

This book contains nearly 450 recipes with a mixture of both vegetarian and nonvegetarian dishes to choose from. You will find recipes for creating savory main dishes, appetizing side dishes, satisfying snacks, and nutritious beverages. You will find recipes for dairy-free smoothies and blender drinks, creamy soups and hearty chowders, delicious curries, stews, and casseroles. If you like desserts, you will find plenty here to choose from, including German Chocolate Cake, Coconut Pecan Pie, and Chocolate Almond Ice Cream.

While this is *not* a low-carb cookbook Every sweet or dessert recipe includes a low sugar version. These recipes use very little sugar or none at all.

*The Coconut Miracle Cookbook* is available from the publisher at www.piccadillybooks.com or from Amazon at https://goo.gl/BGXdii.

**COOKING WITH COCONUT FLOUR**
**A Delicious Low-Carb, Gluten-Free Alternative to Wheat**

*By Bruce Fife, N.D.*

Do you love breads, cakes, pies, cookies, and other wheat products but can't eat them because you are allergic to wheat or sensitive to gluten? Perhaps you avoid wheat because you are concerned about your weight and need to cut down on carbohydrates. If so, the solution for you is coconut flour. Coconut flour is a delicious, healthy alternative to wheat. It is high in fiber, low in digestible carbohydrate, and a good source of protein. It contains no gluten so it is ideal for those with celiac disease.

Coconut flour can be used to make a variety of delicious baked goods, snacks, desserts, and main dishes. It is the only flour used in most of the recipes in this book. These recipes are so delicious that you won't be able to tell that they aren't made with wheat. If you like foods such as German chocolate cake, apple pie, blueberry muffins, cheese crackers, and chicken pot pie, but don't want the wheat, you will love the recipes in this book!

These recipes are designed with your health in mind. Every recipe is completely free of wheat, gluten, soy, trans fats, and artificial sweeteners. Coconut is naturally low in carbohydrate and recipes include both regular and reduced sugar versions.

*Cooking with Coconut Flour* is available from the publisher at www.piccadillybooks.com or from Amazon at https://goo.gl/Qj1xi9 .

## THE COCONUT FLOUR GOURMET
### 150 Delicious Gluten-Free Coconut Flour Recipes
*By Bruce and Leslie Fife*

Is it possible to have great tasting gluten-free foods? Yes, with the secret of coconut flour. Coconut flour is completely gluten-free and is an excellent source of vitamins and minerals and contains about the same amount of protein as whole wheat. The best part is that it tastes fantastic!

Using the basic yeast dough recipe described in this book, you will be able to make gluten-free yeast breads that will remind you of your mother's homemade baked bread. Yet these recipes are easier and quicker to make. With coconut flour and a few other key ingredients, you can make gourmet dinner rolls, sandwich bread, pizza crust, calzones, hamburger and hot dog buns, breadsticks, scones, tortillas, and a variety of artisan breads.

The recipes in this book are designed to appeal to a wide range of tastes. For breakfast you will find a variety of sweet and savory muffins, pancakes, and waffles. The Jalapeno Cheese Muffins and the Ham and Cheese Waffles are incredible! If you like sweets and desserts, you will find cakes, cupcakes, tarts, cookies, and even ice cream sandwiches. You will also find plenty of savory items such as Sesame Pecan Chicken, Tempura Shrimp, Cashew Chicken, Cajun Chicken

Fingers, Sweet and Sour Pork, and even a delicious gluten-free Turkey Dressing. Who knew gluten-free cooking could taste so good?

*The Coconut Flour Gourmet* is available from the publisher at www.piccadillybooks.com or from Amazon at https://amzn.to/2JYAlpT .

## THE COCONUT KETOGENIC DIET
### Supercharge Your Metabolism, Revitalize Thyroid Function, and Lose Excess Weight
*By Bruce Fife, ND*

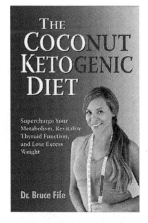

You can enjoy eating rich, full-fat foods and lose weight without counting calories or suffering from hunger. The secret is a high-fat, ketogenic diet. Our bodies need fat. It's necessary for optimal health. It's also necessary in order to lose weight safely and naturally.

Low-fat diets have been heavily promoted for the past three decades, and as a result we are fatter now than ever before. Obviously, there is something wrong with the low-fat approach to weight loss. This book exposes many common myths and misconceptions about fats and weight loss and explains why low-fat diets don't work. It also reveals new, cutting-edge research on one of the world's most exciting weight loss aids—coconut oil—and how you can use it to power up your metabolism, boost your energy, improve thyroid function, and lose unwanted weight.

This revolutionary weight loss program is designed to keep you both slim and healthy using wholesome, natural foods, and the most health-promoting fats. It has proven successful in helping those suffering from obesity, diabetes, heart and circulatory problems, low thyroid function, chronic fatigue, high blood pressure, high cholesterol, and many other conditions.

In this book you will learn: why you need to eat fat to lose fat; why you should not eat lean protein without a source of fat; how to lose weight without feeling hungry or miserable; how to stop food cravings dead cold; how to use your diet to overcome common health problems; how to reach your ideal weight and stay there; why eating rich, delicious foods can help you lose weight; and which foods are the real troublemakers and how to avoid them.

*The Coconut Ketogenic Diets* is available from the publisher at www.piccadillybooks.com or from Amazon at https://goo. gl/cquUCV.

## KETONE THERAPY
### The Ketogenic Cleanse and Anti-Aging Diet
*By Bruce Fife, ND*

The ketogenic diet is one that is very low in carbohydrate, high in fat, with moderate protein. This diet shifts the body into a natural, healthy metabolic state known as nutritional ketosis.

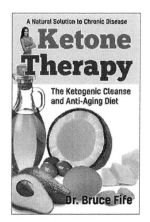

In ketosis the body uses fat as its primary source of energy instead of glucose. Some of this fat is converted into an alternative form of fuel called ketones. Ketones are high-potency fuel that boost energy and cellular efficiency and activates special enzymes that regulate cell survival, repair, and growth. When a person is in nutritional ketosis, blood levels of ketones are elevated to therapeutic levels. In response, high blood pressure drops, cholesterol levels improve, inflammation is reduced, blood sugar levels normalize, and overall health improves.

Low-fat diets have been heavily promoted for the past several decades as the answer to obesity and chronic disease. However, we are fatter and sicker now more than ever before. Obviously, the low-fat approach has not worked. Our bodies actually need fat for optimal health and function more efficiently using fat for fuel.

In this book, you will discover how people are successfully using the ketogenic diet to prevent and treat chronic and degenerative disease. Ketone therapy is backed by decades of medical and clinical research, which has proven the method to be both safe and effective for the treatment of variety of health issues. Topics covered include neurodegenerative disorders, neurodevelopmental disorders, diabetes and metabolic syndrome, detoxification and immune function, digestive disorders, cancer, and much more.

Many health problems that medical science has deemed incurable or untreatable are being reversed. Medications that were once relied on daily are no longer necessary and are being tossed away. People are discovering that a simple, but revolutionary diet based on wholesome, natural foods and the most health-promoting fats is dramatically changing their lives.

*Ketone Therapy* is available from the publisher at www.piccadillybooks.com or from Amazon at https://goo.gl/A7NrhM.

**STOP ALZHEIMER'S NOW!**
**How to Prevent and Reverse Dementia, Parkinson's, ALS, Multiple Sclerosis, and Other Neurodegenerative Disorders**
*By Bruce Fife, ND*
*Foreword by Russell L. Blaylock, MD*

More than 35 million people have dementia today. Alzheimer's disease is the most common form of dementia. Millions more suffer with other neurodegenerative disorders. The number of people affected by these destructive diseases continues to increase every year.

The brain is fully capable of functioning normally for a lifetime, regardless of how long a person lives. While aging is a risk factor for neurodegeneration, it is not the cause! Dementia and other neurodegenerative disorders are disease processes that can be prevented and successfully treated.

This book outlines a program using ketone therapy and diet that is backed by decades of medical and clinical research and has proven successful in restoring mental function and improving both brain and overall health. You will learn how to prevent and even reverse symptoms associated with Alzheimer's disease, Parkinson's disease, amyotrophic lateral sclerosis (ALS), multiple sclerosis (MS), Huntington's disease, epilepsy, diabetes, stroke, and various forms of dementia.

The information in this book is also useful for anyone who wants to be spared from encountering these devastating afflictions. These diseases don't happen overnight. They take years, often decades, to develop.

You *can* stop Alzheimer's and other neurodegenerative diseases now before they take over your life.

"A must read for everyone concerned with Alzheimer's disease...the author explains how diet modifications and the addition of coconut oil can drastically change the course of the disease."
Edmond Devroey, MD
The Longevity Institute

"*Stop Alzheimer's Now!*...will not only be beneficial for Alzheimer's but also for a wide variety of other diseases. I strongly recommend reading this book!"
Sofie Hexebert, MD, PhD

*Stop Alzheimer's Now!* is available from the publisher at www.piccadillybooks.com or from Amazon at https://goo.gl/2t44Ez.


**STOP VISION LOSS NOW!**
**Prevent and Heal Cataracts, Glaucoma, Macular Degeneration, and Other Common Eye Disorders**

*By Bruce Fife, ND*

Losing your eyesight is a frightening thought. Yet, every five seconds someone in the world goes blind. Most causes of visual impairment are caused by age-related diseases such as cataracts, glaucoma, macular degeneration, and diabetic retinopathy. Modern medicine has no cure for these conditions. Treatment usually involves managing the 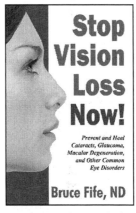 symptoms and attempting to slow the progression of the disease. In some cases surgery is an option, but there is

129

always the danger of adverse side effects that can damage the eyes even further.

Most chronic progressive eye disorders are considered incurable, hopeless. However, there is a successful treatment. It doesn't involve surgery, drugs, or invasive medical procedures. All that is needed is a proper diet. The key is coconut, specifically coconut oil, combined with a low-carb or ketogenic diet. The author used this method to cure is own glaucoma, something standard medical therapy is unable to do.

The coconut based dietary program described in this book has the potential to help prevent and treat many common visual problems including the following: cataracts, glaucoma, macular degeneration, diabetic retinopathy, dry eye syndrome, Sjogren's syndrome, optic neuritis, irritated eyes, conjunctivitis (pink eye), and eye disorders related to neurodegenerative disease (Alzheimer's, Parkinson's, stroke, MS).

Most chronic eye disorders come without warning. No one can tell who will develop a visual handicap as they age. Everybody is at risk. Once the disease is present, treatment is a lifelong process. The best solution is prevention.

In this book, you will learn the basic underlying causes for the most common degenerative eye disorders and what you can do to prevent, stop, and even reverse them.

"Well-researched, comprehensive, and interesting. Dr. Fife has a gift for making advanced nutrition concepts and physiological processes easy for the average reader to understand...There are many personal accounts throughout the book, including the author's story of how he reversed his own early-stage glaucoma."

Franziska Spritzler, RD, CDE

"Skeptical that treating my eyes with the suggestions outlined in this book, I nevertheless began to do them. I have been virtually stunned that just after 2 weeks..the pain in both eyes is completely gone, the scratchy feelings, eye fatigue, and eye dryness are now a thing of the past...My recovery is real, and I have been able to return full time to using my computer."

Maria Atwood, *Wise Traditions*, Weston A. Price Foundation.

***Stop Vision Loss Now!*** is available from the publisher at www.piccadillybooks.com or from Amazon at https://goo.gl/LbQYL9.

## STOP AUTISM NOW!
### A Parent's Guide to Preventing and Reversing Autism Spectrum Disorders
*By Bruce Fife, ND*

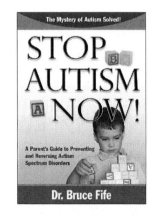

Over 1 million people have autism. This number is rapidly growing. Over the past several years autism has increased to epidemic proportions. Thirty years ago it affected only 1 in 2,500; today 1 out of every 50 children in the United States is affected.

Over the past 12 years there has been a 17 percent increase in childhood developmental disabilities of all types including autism, attention deficit hyperactivity disorder (ADHD), epilepsy, mental retardation, and others. Currently in the United States, 4 million children have ADHD, the most common learning disability, and an incredible one in six children are classified as learning disabled.

Why the sudden astronomical rise in developmental disabilities? Most doctors have no clue what causes autism, nor any idea how to prevent or treat it. The only medically recognized form of treatment is an attempt to teach affected children how to manage the disorder and live with it. Antidepressants, antipsychotics, and stimulants are often prescribed to help them cope with their symptoms. No possibility of a cure is offered, as the condition is considered hopeless.

Autism, however, is not a hopeless condition. It can be prevented and successfully treated without the use of drugs. This book describes an innovative new dietary and lifestyle approach involving coconut ketone therapy that has proven very successful in reversing even some of the most severe developmental disorders, allowing once disabled children to enter regular school and lead normal, happy, productive lives. There is a solution. You can stop autism now!

"Autism is a subject that I have spent a good deal of time analyzing, researching, and writing about and no one does a better job condensing and explaining what is known about this terrible disorder than does Doctor Fife. His advice, designed to treat this disorder, is based on good science and practical experience."
Russell L. Blaylock, MD
Board Certified Neurosurgeon
Author of *Excitotoxins: The Taste That Kills*

**Stop Autism Now!** is available from the publisher at www.piccadillybooks.com or from Amazon at https://goo.gl/Mk1urP.

## FAT HEALS, SUGAR KILLS
## The Cause of and Cure to Cardiovascular Disease, Diabetes, Obesity, and Other Metabolic Disorders
*By Bruce Fife, ND*

For decades we've been avoiding fat like the plague, eating low-fat this, non-fat that, choosing egg whites over the yokes, and trimming off every morsel of fat from meat in order to comply with the *US Dietary Guidelines* recommendation to reduce our fat intake.

The Cause of and Cure for Cardiovascular Disease, Diabetes, Obesity, and Other Metabolic Disorders

**Dr. Bruce Fife**

As a whole, we have succeeded in reducing our total fat intake and replacing it with more so-called "healthy" carbohydrates— most notably refined grains and sugar. What has been the consequence? Obesity is at an all-time high, diabetes and metabolic disorders have increased to epidemic proportions. Heart disease is still our number one killer. We have dutifully followed the advice of the "experts" and as a result, we are sicker now more than ever before.

What went wrong? You can give thanks to the sugar industry. Through clever marketing, misdirection, flawed science, and powerful lobbying, the sugar industry succeeded in diverting attention away from themselves and putting the blame on fat, particularly saturated fat. We fell for it hook, line, and sinker.

Replacing fat with refined carbohydrates was the worse dietary blunder of the 20th century and has led to the skyrocketing levels of chronic disease we are experiencing today. Fortunately, there is a solution—cut out the refined carbohydrates and add good fats back into the diet. New research is showing that fats are essential nutrients with important functions and can be used to help prevent and even reverse heart disease, diabetes, cancer, Alzheimer's, and many other chronic degenerative diseases that are caused by or made worse by the overconsumption of refined carbohydrates. This book explains how sugar and refined carbohydrates are destroying our health. It also reveals new evidence and cutting-edge science behind the incredible healing potential of dietary fats and explains how and why certain fats are now considered not only healthy, but some of our most powerful superfoods.

***Fat Heals, Sugar Kills*** is available from the publisher at www.piccadillybooks.com or from Amazon at https://amzn.to/2WlCDqA.

# About the Author
### Bruce Fife, CN, ND

Dr. Bruce Fife, CN, ND is an author, speaker, certified nutritionist, and naturopathic physician—a physician that uses diet, nutrition, exercise, physical therapy, and other non-drug and non-invasive therapies to treat patients. He has written more than 25 books on diet, nutrition, and healthy fats. Some of his books include: *The Coconut Oil Miracle, Coconut Cures*, and *Stop Alzheimer's Now*. He is the publisher and editor of the *Healthy Ways Newsletter* and serves as the president of the Coconut Research Center (http://www. coconutresearchcenter.org/), a non-profit organization whose purpose is to educate the public and medical community about the health and nutritional aspects of coconut.

Dr. Fife is recognized internationally as the foremost authority on the health and nutritional aspects of coconut and related topics. Dr. Fife was the first to gather together the medical research on the health benefits of coconut oil and present it in an understandable and readable format for the general public. As such, he travels throughout the world educating medical professionals and laypeople alike on the wonders of coconut. For this reason, he is often referred to as the "Coconut Guru" and many respectfully can him "Dr. Coconut."

To view a sample copy of Dr. Fife's *Healthy Ways Newsletter* or to sign-up for a free subscription go to http:// www.coconutresearchcenter.org/?page_id=1917.

# References

**Chapter 2: 1001 Uses for Coconut Oil**
1. https://themaghrebtimes.com/04/13/coconut-oil-is-better-than-any-toothpaste-according-to-study/
2. Hassanali, S. Cola survives on coconuts, rain water. Trinidad Guardian, Aug 9, 2012.
3. Reger, M.A., et al. Effects of beta-hydroxybutyrate on cognition in memory-impaired adults. *Neurobiol Aging* 2004;25:311-314.

**Chapter 3: A Sustainable Natural Resource**
1. Latham, JR, et al. Transformation-induced mutations in transgenic plants: analysis and biosafety implications. *Biotechnol Genet Eng Rev* 2006;23:209-237.
2. Bohn, T, et al. Compositional differences in soybeans on the market: glyphosate accumulates in Roundup Ready GM soybeans. *Food Chem* 2014;15:207-215.
3. Gasnier, C, et al. Glyphosate-based herbicides are toxic and endocrine distruptors in human cell lines. *Toxicology* 2009;262:184-191.
4. https://www.geneticliteracyproject.org/2014/03/05/controversial-iowa-farmer-howard-vlieger-makes-case-against-gmos/

5. www.GMOjudycarman.org

6. Carman, JA, et al. A long-term toxicology study on pigs fed a combined genetically modified (GM) soy and GM maize diet. *Journal of Organic System* 2013;8:38-54.

7. Seralini, G-E, et al. Long term toxicity of a roundup herbicide and a roundup-tolerant genetically modified maize. *Food and Chemical Toxicology* 2012;50:4221-4231.

**Chapter 4: A Clean All-Purpose Industrial Oil**

1. Anonymous. Coconut oil as alternative fuel. *Alexander's Gas & Oil Connections*. Sep 16, 2005.

2. Machacon, H.T.C., et al. The effect of coconut oil and diesel fuel blends on diesel engine performance and exhaust emissions. *JSAE Review* 2001;22:349-355.

3. Tan, R., et al. Carbon balance implications of coconut biodiesel utilization in the Philippine automotive transport sector. *Biomass & Bioenergy* 2004;26:579.

Visit Us on the Web

**P**
**B** Piccadilly Books, Ltd.

www.piccadillybooks.com

Made in the USA
Columbia, SC
14 March 2022

57452365R00076